● A D E R I N S O L A ●

SPACE FOR A CAT

J N WOOD

● D O N O T R E M O V E T H I S P A N E L ●

Text, illustrations and cover design copyright © 2021 J N Wood

All Rights Reserved

For my baby girl

SPACE FOR A CAT

CHAPTER ONE

SPACE DWELLING FAMILY

J N WOOD

'Worky work time for me,' Morrie said, before bending over to kiss Ayla on the top of her head, his beard tickling her scalp. 'Farewell my beautiful daughter. Have a good day at school. Love you.'

Ayla rolled her eyes and scratched the new itch on her head. 'Farewell my father,' she replied. 'Love you too, Dad.'

'HEY!' he exclaimed. 'What

happened to calling me Daddy?'

'I'm seven now,' Ayla replied. 'I shouldn't be calling you Mummy and Daddy anymore. Mum and Dad will suffice.'

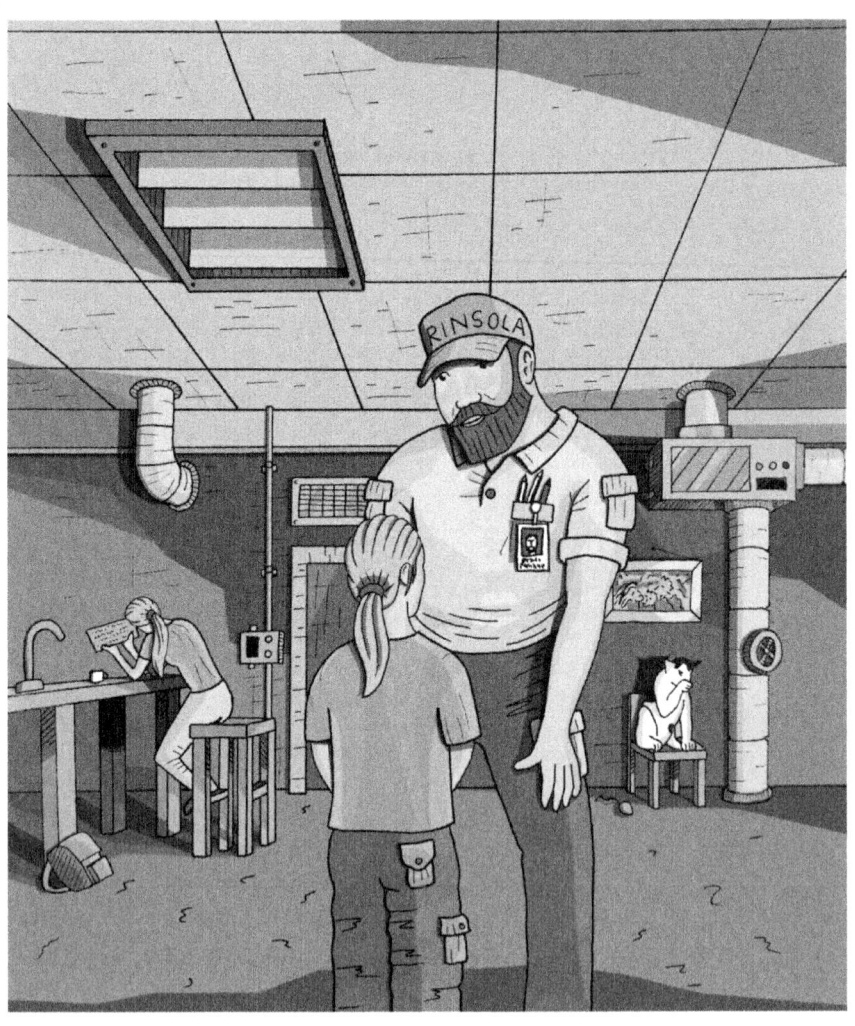

Morrie started backing away towards the door, a big grin forming on his face. 'It will suffice will it?' he asked. 'Could you reconsider that decision please? I'd still like to be called Daddy.' He opened the door and stepped into the corridor outside. 'And don't go down to the lower decks after school.' The front door closed with a loud clang, cutting off Ayla's next words.

'But . . .' she started.

'Your father is right,' Kyra said, not taking her eyes from the tablet device in her hand. 'You shouldn't be going down to the lower decks. It's a very dangerous place for little kids to be running around.'

'You should tell Teddy that, Mummy,' Ayla replied, and then shook her head. 'I mean Mum. It's always his idea to go down there.'

Kyra frowned. 'Teddy is a cat,' she said. 'He wouldn't understand what I was saying.'

Ayla pointed at her large, furry friend. Teddy was sat on a small chair in the corner of their living quarters. 'He's just there, Mum. You shouldn't talk about him like that.'

Kyra sighed and turned to look at Teddy. The cat licked a white paw before furiously rubbing it across the tabby side of his face. 'He's barely aware of my presence, so I don't think I've insulted him.'

'Look how angry he is,' Ayla insisted. 'He understands everything you're saying.'

Kyra put her tablet down and dropped to one knee in front of her daughter. Gently grasping Ayla's shoulders, Kyra said, 'Promise me you won't go down to the lower decks. If there is an emergency, I need you to be close to me.'

'What kind of emergency?' Ayla asked, her eyes widening in alarm.

Kyra smiled reassuringly. 'Don't worry. It's very unlikely anything bad will happen, but you know it can be dangerous sometimes in space. If something unexpected does happen, it's reassuring to know I'd be able to quickly find you.'

'Okay I promise,' Ayla sighed, before pointing at the white and tabby coloured cat. 'Tell Teddy as well please, because he doesn't listen to me.'

Kyra swivelled around until she faced the cat. 'Teddy,' she announced, the tone of her voice making the cat pause mid-lick. His tongue was left hanging out from his mouth. 'Please don't take Ayla down to the lower decks. Okay?'

Teddy's emerald eyes were locked onto Kyra's face as he slurped his tongue back into his mouth.

Kyra smiled apologetically at the feline, thinking he probably assumed the attention meant it was feeding time. She turned back to her daughter. 'I've told him, so neither of you has an excuse. Now let's get you ready for school.'

Ayla had been ready to leave for ten minutes. She'd been waiting for her mum to finish writing her last minute report. 'I just need to pick up my bag,' she said, 'and then I'm ready to go.'

Kyra grinned at her daughter. 'What are we waiting for then? Let's go.'

'Can Teddy come?' Ayla asked.

'I don't think you have much choice. He'll go with you if he wants to.'

Their home was on board an exploration vessel named the Aderinsola, having boarded the huge chunk of metal shortly after Ayla was born.

The ship had covered many light years in the intervening years, and was currently flying through the Triangulum Galaxy, an incredibly long way from Earth in the Milky Way Galaxy. Ayla knew that her mum and dad were very clever. They were physicists, and along with the other scientists living on board the Aderinsola, they studied the many secrets held within this galaxy.

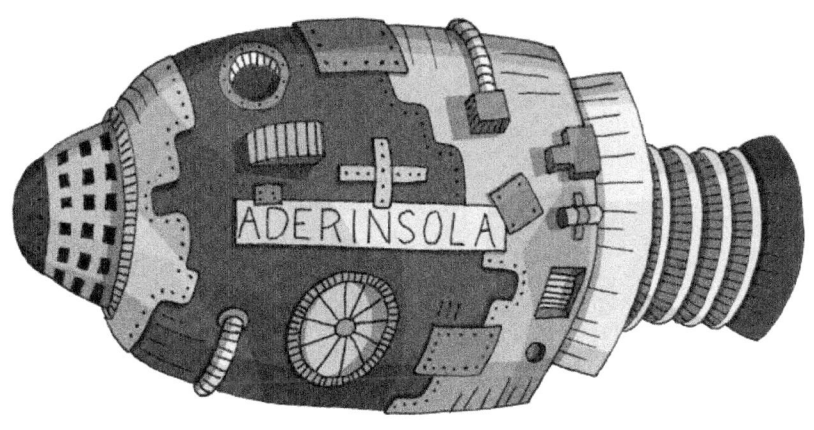

Ayla held her mum's hand as they walked side by side through one of the ship's many corridors. Teddy was darting between Kyra and her daughter, leaping into the air before pouncing on Ayla's shadow.

'Why are the lower decks so dangerous?' Ayla asked.

'The lower decks weren't designed for children to play in,' Kyra explained. 'The engines are down there, so it's dirty and loud. It's safer up here on the habitat decks.'

'Is that why Teddy always has dirty paws?'

'I expect so, and probably the reason why your clothes are always so dirty,' Kyra answered.

'I don't have dirty clothes,' Ayla exclaimed, offended by her mother's comment.

Kyra opened her mouth to respond, but closed it when she saw the father of one of Ayla's classmates walking towards them. She returned his smile and nodded as he passed, before looking down at her daughter. 'Your clothes are always dirty after you've been to the lower decks.'

'Why is there never anyone else down there?' Ayla asked.

'It's a modern engine,' Kyra replied. 'The good ones almost maintain themselves nowadays.'

Kyra stopped them outside the entrance to the school, with Teddy sticking close to Ayla's side.

'I think Teddy is going to school with you,' Kyra said. 'Just make sure he isn't a nuisance, and tell Miss Johnson to call me if she wants me to pick him up. Give me a hug please.'

Kyra dropped to one knee so Ayla could wrap her arms around her mum's neck. Teddy immediately started to play with Kyra's hair.

'Teddy, don't do that please,' Kyra moaned.

'He's only saying goodbye,' Ayla said, as she stepped back from her mum.

'I very much doubt that,' Kyra said. 'I think he just likes to pull my hair out. You two have a good day at school, and go straight home when you've finished. I should be home by the time you get back. I love you, Baby Girl.'

Ayla sighed at the "Baby Girl" name. 'Love you too, Mummy,' she said, before spinning around and walking towards the entrance, with Teddy close behind. 'I meant Mum,' Ayla said over shoulder, 'not Mummy.'

Kyra smiled, hoping her daughter wouldn't grow up too soon.

CHAPTER TWO

SCHOOL GOSSIP

'AYLA!!!' Miss Johnson called out. 'Cat on the floor please, otherwise your mother will be coming to get him.'

Teddy was sprawled on his back, taking up most of Ayla's desk. He was fast asleep, with his white belly on display. Ayla had been finding it difficult to read the text on her display, as the big cat blocked most of it.

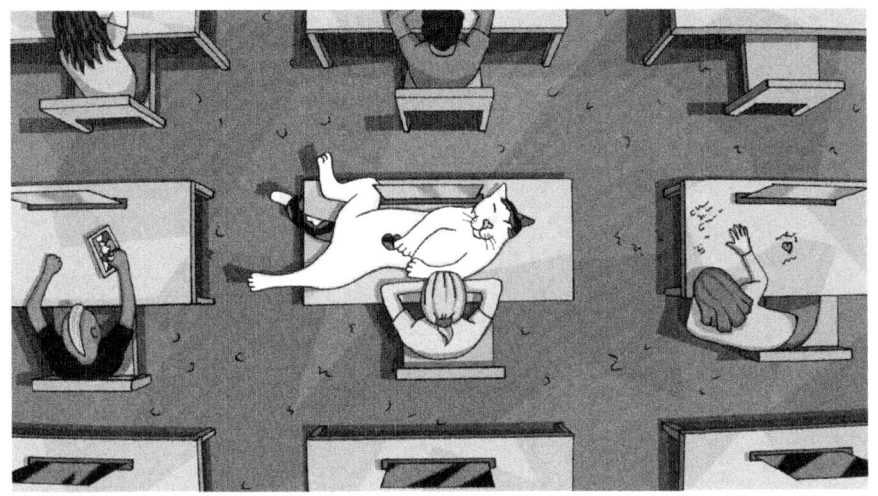

Ayla's classmates all turned to look at them as she struggled to pick Teddy up and place him on the floor. The cat looked irritated at the sudden disturbance, but was soon curled up under the desk, lying on Ayla's feet.

Ayla's desk was positioned in the middle of the room, surrounded by nineteen other children. They were all around her age. Kiki was the oldest in the class at nine years old. She was a good friend of Ayla, but would soon be moving up to the next age group.

Kiki leaned closer to Ayla, filling the small gap separating their desks. 'My dad told me a story about doggy space ships last night,' she whispered.

Ayla felt Teddy move at Kiki's words. She looked down to find his ears pointing straight up. 'What do you mean?' she asked Kiki.

Kiki glanced to the front of the room, where Miss Johnson was sat behind her desk. She had her head buried in the pages of a book, the same story Ayla and Kiki were supposed to be reading on their computer displays. She turned her attention back to Ayla. 'My dad said there are space ships that have flight crews made up of dogs, well . . . they aren't called dogs in this galaxy. They're called boomgaboons.'

'Boomgaboons,' Ayla whispered. 'That's just a made-up word.'

Kiki shook her head. 'My dad said that's what dogs are called in the Triangulum Galaxy. They are really intelligent and can fly space ships. They fly around searching for gongadims.'

'What are gongadims?' Ayla asked.

Kiki leaned closer to Ayla so the two girls' shoulders were almost touching. 'Cats,' she whispered.

Ayla let out a high-pitched shriek when Teddy's front paws suddenly landed on her lap, as he rubbed his face against her arm.

'AYLA AND KIKI!!!' Miss Johnson yelled. 'If you've finished the chapter already, maybe one of you would like to summarise it for the rest of the class.'

'We haven't finished yet, Miss,' Kiki replied, as she quickly shifted her weight back onto her chair. 'I noticed Teddy had something sticking out of his paw, so I was just telling Ayla about it.'

'Ayla Morrison,' Miss Johnson said with a scowl. 'If I have to talk about that cat one more time, I'm calling your mother.'

'Yes, Miss,' Ayla said as she gently pushed down on Teddy's back, trying to get him to relax and sit on the floor.

SPACE FOR A CAT

CHAPTER THREE

GRAB THAT CAT

J N WOOD

The school day was finally over, and Ayla slowly walked alongside Kiki. Ayla was mightily relieved that Teddy hadn't tried taking them to the lower decks. She figured the cat must have realised how serious Mum had been at breakfast. Teddy weaved between the two girls, occasionally tripping one of them if they weren't paying attention to the cat's rapid movements.

'Tell me about the dog ships,' Ayla requested.

'My dad said there is a planet near here like Earth, but instead of humans, creatures that look exactly like dogs are the top dog.' Kiki laughed and elbowed Ayla in her ribs. **'HE HE HA HA!** Do you get it?' she asked. 'The dogs are the top dog.'

Ayla understood the joke but she didn't find it that funny. She laughed along with her friend anyway. **'HA HA HA.'**

'My dad is funny,' Kiki chuckled.

'What did you say the dog creatures were called?' Ayla asked.

'Boomgaboons,' Kiki replied, 'and the species that look like cats are called gongadims.'

Ayla didn't believe a word Kiki was saying. How could there possibly be creatures that look exactly like cats and dogs living all the way out here? 'Do you think your dad was joking when he told you about them?' she asked.

'Nope,' Kiki replied, shaking her head. 'He was being totally serious.'

A loud automated voice suddenly bellowed through the ship.

'PROXIMITY ALERT!!! PROXIMITY ALERT!!!'

Ayla frantically looked around for Teddy, finding he was already at her side. He stared up at her with concern in his eyes.

'ALL FLIGHT CREW TO RETURN TO THEIR STATIONS IMMEDIATELY!!! PASSENGERS MUST RETURN TO THEIR CABINS!!!'

'Not another one,' Kiki said, sounding exasperated.

'We haven't heard an alert like that for ages,' Ayla said, finding she was holding Kiki's arm for comfort.

'True, but we used to get them all the time.' Kiki gently patted Ayla's hand and pulled her arm away. 'I need to get back to my cabin. You better go too. See you at school tomorrow.'

Ayla watched Kiki turn and move away from her, before looking down at Teddy. 'Shall we run home?' she asked her feline friend.

Teddy glanced in the direction of their cabin and then back up to Ayla's face. She could tell he was worried.

'I'm glad you agree,' Ayla said. 'Let's go.' She started running with Teddy close by her side. He was a much faster runner than his human sister, but he wanted to make sure she was safe.

A different voice boomed through the speakers dotted throughout the ship.

'THIS IS CAPTAIN SHIRIN. IF YOU'RE NOT ALREADY STRAPPED IN, HOLD ON TO SOMETHING. THE SHIP WILL BE MAKING EVASIVE MANOEUVRES VERY SOON.'

Ayla's instant reaction was to hold onto her cat. When they were agonisingly close to each other, she was pulled away from him and hurled into the air.

Teddy was thrown in the opposite direction. **'MEEEEEOWWWW!'** he screeched.

Ayla swung her arms and kicked her legs, desperately trying to swim back to Teddy. A split second later they were both slammed back down to the floor, knocking the breath from Ayla's lungs. She started to crawl towards Teddy, who was also trying to move closer to her. Yet again, they were cruelly ripped from each other's grasp and flung into the air. Ayla was spun around so she could no longer see her cat, but then a strong arm was wrapped around her middle.

'IT'S OKAY, BABY GIRL!' her dad shouted. **'I'VE GOT YOU!'**

'DADDY!' Ayla yelled. **'WE NEED TO GET TEDDY!'**

'Don't worry I've got him,' Morrie replied, as he kicked off from the wall behind him, propelling them to the opposite wall. 'I should probably say that he's got me. His claws are digging into my back.'

Morrie stopped them hitting the wall with an outstretched hand, before pulling a handle. A large metal panel sprung from the wall and flew across the corridor, loudly bouncing across the floor. Six emergency safety chairs unfolded and Morrie strapped himself into the closest one. He sat Ayla on the chair next to him and pulled the safety belts over her shoulders, quickly clipping them into place. Teddy had made his way down to Morrie's lap, and was now stretching his front legs out towards Ayla.

'Teddy, it's okay,' Ayla said, and reached out for her cat. 'Can I have him, Daddy?'

'You need to hold on tight to him,' Morrie warned, allowing the cat to step over and almost block his daughter from sight.

'Where's Mummy?' Ayla asked, as Teddy pressed his face into her chest.

'She's safe,' her dad replied. 'I spoke to her two minutes ago. Don't worry, it'll be over soon.'

'What's happening?' Ayla asked.

'The evasive manoeuvres are playing havoc with the artificial gravity. Once we're clear of the asteroids, hopefully the ship will settle down.'

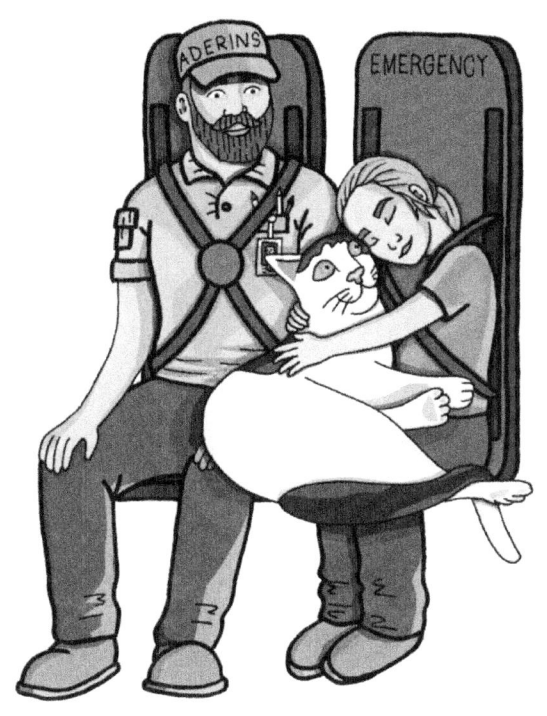

As soon as Morrie had stopped speaking, the ship calmed down just like he'd said. Ayla noticed the insides of her belly now seemed to be still.

'THIS IS CAPTAIN SHIRIN AGAIN. SORRY ABOUT THAT FOLKS. WE'RE ALL CLEAR

NOW. PLEASE MAKE THE MEDICAL STAFF AWARE IF ANYONE REQUIRES ATTENTION.'

Morrie unclipped his safety belt before doing the same with Ayla's. 'We should get back to your mum. She'll be worried sick.'

'Is it really over?' Ayla asked.

'Yeah we'll be fine now. The captain will let us know if things change.' Morrie knelt down and took Ayla's face in his hands, inspecting every little bit of her. 'Are you okay? Does it hurt anywhere?'

Ayla smiled, trying to reassure her worried father. 'I'm fine, Dad. I was winded when I hit the floor, but I'm okay now.'

Teddy rubbed himself up against Morrie's leg, drawing his attention down to the cat. He stroked a hand across Teddy's head and all the way down his back, not stopping until he reached the tip of his tail. 'Are you okay, Teddy?' Morrie asked.

Teddy replied with a reverberating purr, so Morrie assumed he must be unharmed.

They walked into their cabin to find Kyra impatiently pacing through the living quarters. Upon seeing Ayla, she ran to her and wrapped her arms around her daughter, lifting her up.

'I was so worried about you,' Kyra said, her face pressed into her daughter's neck.

'I'm okay, Mummy. I was worried about you. I had Daddy and Teddy, but you were all alone.'

Kyra leaned her face away from Ayla's. 'I was safely strapped into one of the emergency chairs in here. No need to worry about me.'

'Teddy stayed with me the entire time, but then we were floating and couldn't reach each other. Daddy appeared from nowhere and scooped me up. He put me in one of the emergency chairs in the corridor.'

Kyra smiled at Morrie, her eyes filling with tears.

Five minutes later, they were all facing a large door. Most of it consisted of glass, but because it was dark on the other side, all Ayla could see was a reflection of herself and her family.

'This is the escape shuttle you should come to if you hear an abandon ship alert,' Kyra instructed.

'I know, Mum,' Ayla sighed. 'You've already told me this, and Miss Johnson has a day talking about this kind of thing at the beginning of every school term.'

'Just think of this as a little refresher course,' Morrie said. 'If anything does happen, we want to be together.'

Ayla was beginning to worry. Her mum and dad had never been this concerned about escape shuttles before. 'Is everything okay?' she asked.

Kyra gently squeezed Ayla's shoulders. 'Everything's fine,' she cheerfully replied. 'I think we should grab something to eat. All that excitement has made me hungry.'

CHAPTER FOUR

BOUNCY BALL

Over the next few days, Teddy grew increasingly bored with merely playing on the habitat decks. Ayla could tell he wanted to go down the gigantic metal stairway and roll around in the dirt. After school one afternoon, Kiki had joined them to play Teddy's favourite game.

'He's like a dog,' Kiki commented, after Ayla had thrown the small bouncy ball for Teddy to retrieve. The cat was happily sprinting after the ball.

'Cats can play fetch if they want to,' Ayla said. 'Why should dogs get to enjoy it and not cats?'

'I didn't say cats weren't allowed to enjoy it,' Kiki replied. 'I just think it's strange. I've never seen it before.'

'Maybe this is what gongadims do,' Ayla suggested.

'Teddy isn't a gongadim,' Kiki insisted. 'He's a cat.'

Teddy was strolling back to them, the black rubber ball held securely in his mouth. He hesitated as he passed the entrance to the metal stairway, before stopping completely after a few more steps. He looked at Ayla, and then back to the entrance.

'Come on, Teddy,' Ayla said. 'Bring the ball back.'

With one brisk shake of his head, the cat released the ball and it flew straight into the stairway. Ayla and Kiki could hear the **BOING**, **BOING** noise as the ball ricocheted off the metal steps. Teddy was frozen to the spot, his attention locked onto Ayla. There was a mischievous glint in his eye.

'You're a very bad cat,' Ayla said as she marched up to him. She pointed a finger at him and wagged it as she walked. 'You've lost your favourite bouncy ball now.'

Before Ayla could say another word, Teddy darted into the stairway and started leaping down the stairs.

'TEDDY!' Ayla shouted.

'I'm not allowed to go down there,' Kiki said.

'I won't be long,' Ayla told her. 'I'll just get Teddy and come straight back.'

'BE CAREFUL!' Kiki called out, as Ayla disappeared into the gloom of the lower decks.

Ayla could see a blur of white fur below her when she leaned out over the edge of the stairs. She continued to yell Teddy's name as she descended, but the cat couldn't be swayed from his important mission to retrieve the lost ball.

Out of breath from the effort, she finally caught up with him when they were three decks down, in the heart of the ship's engine. The cat was sat with the ball in his mouth, waiting expectantly for his favourite human.

'You know we can't come down here,' she scolded. 'Mum will be really angry if she finds out.'

Teddy rolled over onto his back, making sure every little bit of him was covered in a layer of grime.

'You better clean yourself before we get home,' Ayla sighed. 'I wish your fur didn't have so much white.'

'PROXIMITY ALERT!!! PROXIMITY ALERT!!!'

'NOT NOW!' Ayla wailed. 'Teddy, no messing around. We need to go back upstairs.'

The cat looked genuinely apologetic as he quickly rose to his feet and sidled up to Ayla.

'It's okay, Teddy,' she said. 'You didn't know there would be another alert.'

They started running up the stairs, but it was much quicker coming down than going back up. Ayla was struggling by the time they got to the next deck, and had to stop to catch her breath. Teddy waited patiently by her side.

'I just need thirty seconds,' Ayla said.

'Meeroww,' Teddy told her. 'Meeerowww, meeroww, merow.'

'Okay I'm ready. Let's go.'

An almighty sound echoed through the ship, making Ayla pause as her foot hit the next step.

BOOOOOOOOOOOOM!!!

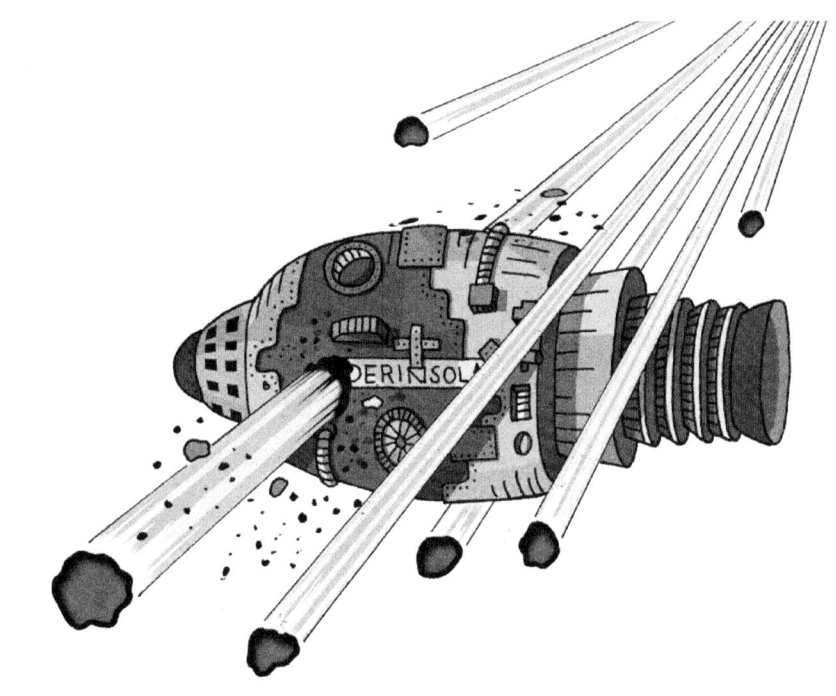

The deafening noise was swiftly followed by a bone shattering shudder. She could feel the almighty tremble as it passed from the metal bannister and into her, shaking her bones as it travelled through her entire body.

The ship's automated voice started speaking again.

'ABANDON SHIP! ABANDON SHIP! ALL FLIGHT CREW AND PASSENGERS ABANDON SHIP! FIND THE NEAREST ESCAPE SHUTTLE AND ABANDON SHIP!!!'

'NOOOOO!!!!' Ayla cried, before starting up the stairs again. Tears were filling her eyes, obscuring her vision. **'WE WON'T BE**

ABLE TO GET TO MUMMY AND DADDY IN TIME!'

The wobble in her legs was increasing as the stairs beneath her feet continued to shake, slowing her progress even further. She tripped on one of the steps, hurting her hands on the sharp metal edges as she fell. Teddy was instantly by her face, prodding her forehead with his nose. She held in the impulse to scream from the pain and clambered to her feet. Teddy quickly leapt up three steps and turned back to look at her, his eyes imploring her to continue. She held her painful hands close to her body and started the long climb again. By the time they got to the entrance to the next deck, she was almost hysterical.

'I CAN'T DO IT, TEDDY!' she wailed, staring at the blood on the palms of her hands. 'THE STAIRS ARE TOO SHAKY!'

She looked down to the metal floor, but couldn't see her cat anywhere. She wiped away the tears with the back of her hand and frantically searched for him. She leaned out over the edge to try and spot him on the stairs above and below.

'MEEEEEEOOOOWAAAARRROOOO!!!'

She spun around and peered into the gloomy entrance next to her. Teddy was standing next to a door, further along the corridor that stretched away. He was almost bouncing up and down on the spot, obviously excited about something.

'WE NEED TO GET TO MUMMY AND DADDY!' she yelled.

'MEEEEEEOOOOWAAAARRROOOO!!!'

'NO TEDDY! WE NEED TO GO!'

The cat stopped bouncing and placed a paw on the door next to him.

'THIS IS THE CAPTAIN SPEAKING. IT IS IMPERITIVE THAT EVERYONE ABANDON SHIP. THE ADERINSOLA HAS SUFFERED CATASTROPHIC DAMAGE FROM AN ASTEROID STRIKE. WE HAVE LESS THAN FIVE MINUTES BEFORE THE ENTIRE SHIP IMPLODES. ABANDON SHIP IMMEDIATELY!!!'

The captain's terrible words forced Ayla's legs to start moving. As she ran towards Teddy, she just wanted her daddy to scoop her up again and keep her safe. 'I hope you've found a shortcut to Mummy and Daddy,' she said.

When she was nearing her cat, she could see he wasn't touching an ordinary door. His paw was resting on the door of an escape shuttle.

'But we need to get to the shuttle Mummy and Daddy told us to use,' she said.

Teddy looked at the door and then back up at Ayla. 'Meeeroooowww.'

'I don't know how to fly an escape shuttle,' she complained.

Teddy walked his front legs up the door until he could reach the emergency release button. He pushed down onto the orange glowing pad with all of his weight, forcing the door to open with a loud hiss. Teddy dropped down so he was halfway inside the shuttle. He looked up at Ayla, his eyes pleading for her to join him.

'But I want to be with Mummy and Daddy.'

'ABANDON SHIP!!! ABANDON SHIP!!!'

Teddy walked inside and jumped up onto one of the chairs. He turned to look at the open door and said, 'Meeearrrroww.'

Ayla knew she had to make a decision soon, because they didn't have much time left. She realised she would have to trust in her best friend.

CHAPTER FIVE

GET OFF THE SHIP!!!

J N WOOD

Ayla sat on the chair next to Teddy, in front of displays lit up with many different colours. 'How do we launch the shuttle?' she asked, studying the array of different symbols on the colourful screen.

The cat leapt from his chair and trotted over to the outer door. He pressed his paw onto a pad inside the shuttle and the door closed. Teddy walked back towards her, the inner door closing behind him. A female voice swiftly followed.

'ALL PASSENGERS MUST TAKE THEIR SEATS IMMEDIATELY. THE SHUTTLE WILL LAUNCH IN THIRTY SECONDS.'

'It must be automatic,' Ayla murmured.

Her dad's voice suddenly filled the shuttle. 'Edwin Morrison to all shuttles. Does anyone have my daughter on board?'

'THAT'S MY DADDY!' Ayla screamed. **'I'M HERE! I'M ON AN ESCAPE SHUTTLE!'**

The responses from the other escaping shuttles came back thick and fast.

'THAT'S A NEGATIVE FROM US MORRIE. WE DON'T HAVE HER IN FIFTY TWO.'

'SORRY, SHE'S NOT WITH US IN SHUTTLE FIFTY SIX.'

'NEGATIVE FROM FORTY ONE.'

'NEGATIVE.'

'NEGATIVE.'

'NEGATIVE.'

'NEGATIVE.'

Ayla pounded her fists into the arms of the chair. **'PLEASE DADDY!!! I'M RIGHT HERE!!!'**

'WE DON'T HAVE HER MORRIE. YOU NEED TO GET OFF THE SHIP ASAP. IT'S BREAKING UP. YOU DON'T HAVE MUCH TIME!!!'

'We're not leaving without our daughter,' Morrie replied.

'GET OFF THE SHIP, DADDY!'

Ayla shouted. She stared at the display through her tears. 'Teddy, what should I do? He can't hear me.'

'AYLA ISN'T WITH US ON SHUTTLE NINE. MORRIE, IS KYRA STILL WITH YOU?'

'I'm still here,' Kyra replied to the man's question. 'We're not leaving without Ayla. Don't even try to convince us otherwise.'

'MUMMY!' Ayla exclaimed. **'GET OFF THE SHIP, MUMMY!'**

Teddy lifted his front paws and rested them on the display in front of him. **'MEROWROW!!!'** he loudly squealed.

'**THAT WAS A CAT!!!**' Kyra screeched. 'All shuttles. Please respond if you have a cat on board?'

None of them answered.

Ayla and Teddy's escape shuttle started talking again.

'**THE SHUTTLE WILL LAUNCH IN TEN . . . NINE . . . EIGHT . . .**'

'**MEROWROW!!!**' Teddy repeated, but much louder this time.

'That's definitely Teddy,' Kyra excitedly said. 'Ayla, are you with Teddy?'

'Can they hear you?' Ayla asked her furry friend.

'**AYLA BABY!!!**' Morrie shouted. '**WE CAN HEAR YOU! WHERE ARE YOU?**'

Ayla whipped her head around to face the display. **'I'M HERE DADDY! I'M ON AN ESCAPE SHUTTLE WITH TEDDY! PLEASE COME AND GET US!'**

Ayla and Teddy were both thrust backwards into their cushioned chairs when the shuttle was jettisoned away from the Aderinsola.

'Don't worry, Baby Girl,' Kyra said. 'We're coming for you. Which shuttle are you in?'

'I don't know,' Ayla replied, 'but I think we just launched.'

'What number shuttle is it?' Morrie asked. 'All of the shuttles are numbered.'

'I don't know, Daddy. Come and get us.'

'MEEEEEOOOOOW!' Teddy yelled.

Ayla turned to look at her cat. His eyes were fixed on her, but then he looked at his display. In the top right hand corner of the screen, the numbers two and four glowed with an orange hue.

'TWENTY FOUR!' Ayla shouted. **'SHUTTLE TWENTY FOUR!'**

'Our shuttle is about to launch,' Kyra told her. 'We're right behind you.'

CHAPTER SIX

DIZZY

J N WOOD

'How much longer are you going to be?' Ayla asked.

'It won't be long,' Kyra replied. 'We're on our way.'

'Ayla,' Morrie said, 'our scanners are picking up more asteroids heading towards you.'

Ayla stared at her display, trying to see whatever her dad was seeing. 'Are they going to hit us?'

'Not if you take control of the shuttle and steer away from them,' Kyra told her.

'I don't know how to do that, Mummy.'

'How many times did I tell the captain we needed to teach the kids how to fly?' Morrie asked his wife.

'Not now Morrie,' Kyra growled.

'Sorry,' Morrie said. 'Ayla, we'll talk you through it. You'll be fine.'

'Thirty seconds,' Kyra whispered.

'Ayla, look at the display in front of you,' Morrie instructed, his words coming through much more rapidly now. 'There should be a little rectangle in the top left that says auto mode.'

Ayla scoured the many words framed by different shapes. **'I CAN'T SEE IT!'** she cried.

'We don't have long,' Kyra said.

Ayla and Teddy's escape shuttle suddenly lurched to the left and then to the right.

'THAT'S IT, BABY GIRL!!!' Morrie yelled. **'YOU HAVE CONTROL!'**

Ayla lifted her hands up into the air. 'I honestly haven't done anything. I'm not controlling it.'

She turned to see Teddy still had his paws on the display in front of him, but they were sliding back and forth across the screen. 'I think Teddy's doing it,' she said.

'That's impossible, Ayla,' Morrie said. 'You must have pressed something by accident.'

'It's not me, Daddy.'

Teddy was indeed doing it. He was trying his best to steer them away from danger, but the shuttle's controls were made for human fingers, not his paws. Even if he'd been human, he didn't think they would have had enough time. He could see the huge field of asteroids on his scanner, and Morrie was right. They were heading straight for them. The amount of rocks was astronomical, so much so the shuttle's 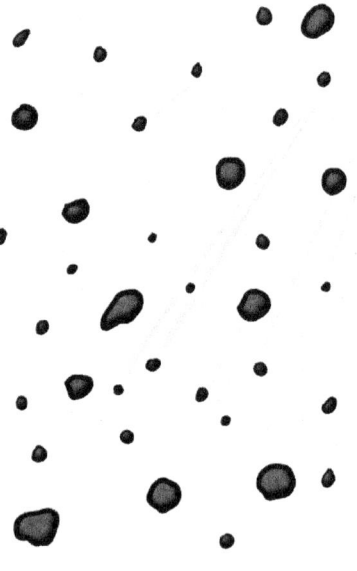 sensors were constantly updating the numbers. At the last count there were **1876 . . . 77 . . . 78 . . . 79.**

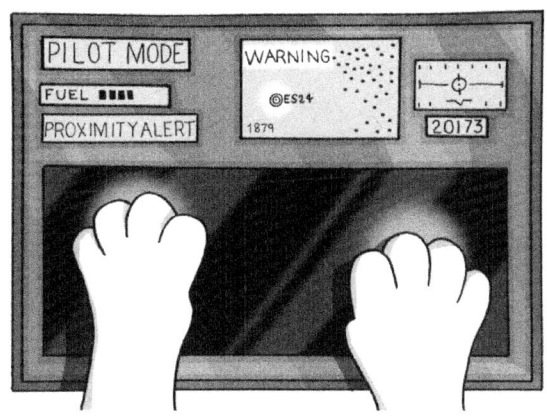

'Just keep doing what you're doing, Baby Girl,' Kyra said. 'You're heading in the right direction.'

'It's not going to be enough,' Morrie whispered.

'What do you mean, Daddy?' Ayla asked.

'Nothing,' Kyra said. 'Daddy was just talking to me. Keep going.'

'You're doing a fantastic job,' Morrie said, his voice starting to crack. 'We love you, Baby Girl.'

'I love you too,' Ayla replied, the fear in her voice matching her father's.

The shuttle suddenly made a series of wild and dramatic turns, hurling Ayla from one side of her chair to the other. Teddy's paws were a blur, rapidly sliding across the screen as they controlled two glowing circles. He was flying them through a massive asteroid strike, expertly avoiding each and every speeding space rock.

'THAT'S IT!' Kyra shouted. **'YOU'RE DOING IT!** Morrie, she's going to make it.'

'MUMMY SAID YOU'RE DOING IT, TEDDY!' Ayla yelled.

'Meow,' was the only thing the cat could say, as all of his attention was needed to control the shuttle.

Teddy saw it too late. An asteroid was going to hit them but he didn't have the time to do anything about it. He felt entirely helpless. He didn't even have time to look at his best friend. The impact when the rock hit the rear end of the shuttle launched Teddy into the air. Ayla screamed, her hands tightly gripping the arms of her chair, otherwise she'd have joined Teddy in the air. The cat was spinning around inside the shuttle, bouncing off the walls and ceiling.

'**AYYYLAAAAA!!!**' Kyra screamed. '**TALK TO US, BABY GIRL!!!**'

'**MUUUUUMMMMMMMYYYYY!!!**' Ayla cried. She was finding it harder and harder to focus on anything in her new revolving world.

'**GO AFTER HER, MORRIE!**' Kyra yelled.

'We can't go into the asteroids,' Morrie replied, the frustration obvious in his voice. 'We have to wait for them to pass.'

Ayla and Teddy's escape shuttle was spinning out of control, travelling at extraordinary speeds. Ayla was so dizzy she felt like she was about to lose consciousness. She could still see a very fuzzy image of Teddy out of the corner of her eye. He'd managed to dig his claws into the ceiling and was now clinging on for dear life, staring down at Ayla. She could tell he was scared, but his eyes also had that apologetic look to them, the expression he had when he  thought he'd done something wrong.

'IT'SSSS OOOOOKAAAAY TEDDYYYY,' she said, now barely able to keep her eyes open. **'YOUUUU DIIIIIID YOURRR BESSSSST.'**

'Don't worry Baby Girl,' Morrie said, his voice becoming fainter and fainter. 'We'll find you.'

'We're coming,' Kyra said. 'We're…'

Then there was only silence.

SPACE FOR A CAT

CHAPTER SEVEN

WHAT'S SO FUNNY?

J N WOOD

Ayla opened her eyes to find she was lying on the floor of the shuttle. She realised she must have slipped off the chair when they were spinning, but couldn't remember it happening. She heard a scratching noise coming from above her, so shifted her body to get a better view of her surroundings. Teddy was sitting on his chair, pawing at the display. She watched him for a few moments, wondering how intelligent her cat really was. It had definitely been him flying the shuttle, and he'd actually been doing a really good job until they were hit. She could tell he wasn't just haphazardly pawing at the display, but more like he had some kind of purpose.

Then she remembered the predicament they were in. Mummy and Daddy would be looking for them. She sat up and rested her back against the base of the chair, trying to calm her fuzzy head. 'What are you doing, Teddy?'

The cat stopped and turned to look at her. He was almost frowning. 'Merow merow meeyuuu merow.'

'I don't know what that means,' she said, and using the chair, managed to get up onto her feet. Her legs still felt very wobbly, so she had to lean heavily on the chair. 'Where are we? Have Mummy and Daddy been trying to speak to us?'

Teddy looked at his display again. 'Meowarooooarrrr.'

Ayla thought that was definitely a no. 'Can you fly us back to them?'

Teddy padded one paw against the display. The words **FUEL** and **EMPTY** flashed on and off.

'Does that mean we can't fly anywhere?' she asked.

Teddy looked back at her with his apologetic expression again.

She sat on the chair and placed her head in her hands. 'What are we going to do?'

Teddy leapt across the gap, landing on her lap and almost knocking her from her chair. She pulled her hands from her face and found his bright emerald eyes staring at her.

'At least I'm not alone,' she murmured.

Both Ayla's and Teddy's screens started flashing red and yellow. Teddy spun around and stretched his front legs up so he could get a closer look at Ayla's display. He prodded the screen with his paw until a message popped up.

UNIDENTIFIED VESSEL APPROACHING

'Is it Mummy and Daddy?' Ayla asked.

'Merumarrowrow,' Teddy answered.

Ayla leaned around the cat so she could see his face. She thought he still looked concerned, meaning he wasn't sure who it may be.

'What should we do?' Ayla asked.

Teddy sighed and dropped down to heavily sit on Ayla's lap.

'Do we just sit and wait?' she asked.

'Meorowrow.'

Five minutes later, there was a loud clunking noise as the unidentified vessel docked with their shuttle.

'I'm scared,' Ayla said, hugging Teddy tight to her chest. She jumped when the shuttle started speaking again.

'THE OUTER AIRLOCK HAS BEEN COMPROMISED. DECOMPRESSION IS NOT IMMINENT BECAUSE A BREATHABLE ATMOSPHERE IS BEING PUMPED INTO THE SHUTTLE. SOMETHING IS NOW TRYING TO GAIN ACCESS TO THE INNER AIRLOCK.'

'That's good isn't it?' Ayla asked. 'The shuttle not decompressing must be a good thing.'

The inner door opened with a loud hiss. Red tinted smoke quickly filled the opening, swirling into the shuttle and obscuring whatever was trying to enter. A person began to slowly emerge, but stopped when they were still mostly enveloped in smoke.

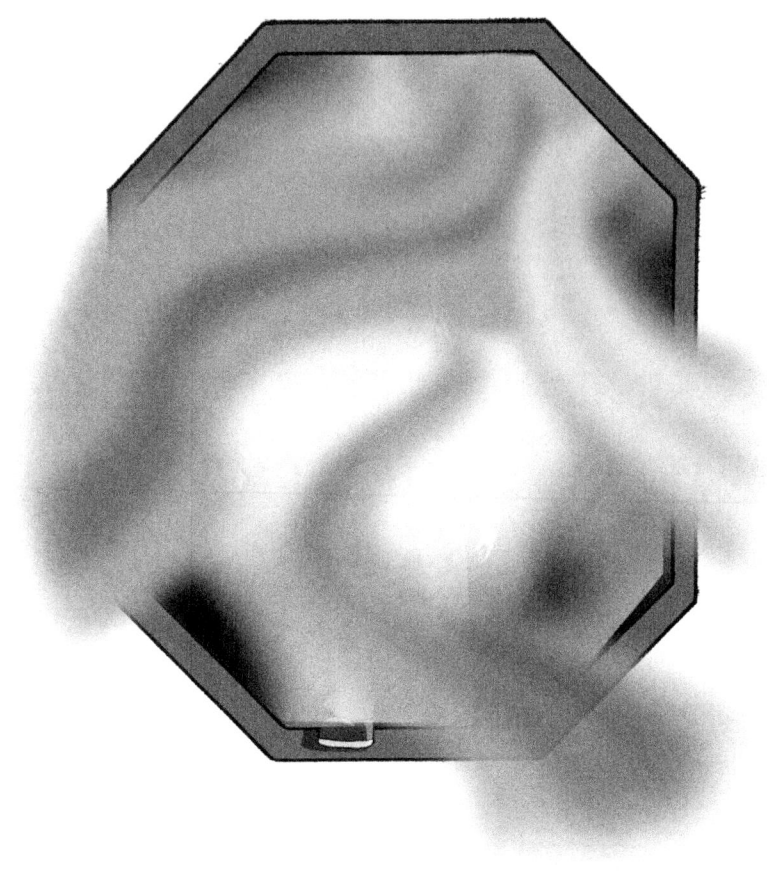

'Who are you and what do you want?' the person asked.

'My name is Ayla. This is . . .'

'THE INNER AIRLOCK HAS BEEN COMPROMISED. DECOMPRESSION IS NOT IMMINENT BECAUSE A BREATHABLE ATMOSPHERE IS BEING PUMPED INTO THE SHUTTLE...'

'SHUTTLE!' Ayla shouted. **'PLEASE BE QUIET!'**

A series of laughs and sniggers emanated from inside the smoke filled vessel.

Ayla shifted, forcing Teddy to drop to the floor. She left the chair and peered into the swirling smoke, trying to see who else was in there. 'My name is Ayla and this is Teddy,' she said, looking down at the cat by her side. 'We just want to go home.'

CHAPTER EIGHT

PROMISES

The person stepped forwards, fully emerging from the mysterious smoke. It was a girl with a big welcoming smile on her face. She looked no older than eleven or twelve. 'Hi Ayla and Teddy,' she said. 'My name is Margo.' She turned slightly and gestured towards her ship. 'Would you like to come on board the Santacruise? We have plenty of food for you both if you're hungry.'

Ayla eyed the girl suspiciously. 'My parents are looking for this shuttle,' she told her. 'We should stay here in case they find it.'

'The Santacruise's computers told me you're out of fuel,' Margo said. 'You can't float around the galaxy for the rest of your lives.'

'We're not going to,' Ayla replied. 'My parents will find us.'

Margo scrunched up her face, looking like she didn't want to say the next words. 'Our computers also told us there are no other ships for hundreds of thousands of miles. I'm sorry, but they're not finding you anytime soon.'

'That can't be right,' Ayla insisted. 'They were following us. They should be here soon.'

'Where are you from?' Margo asked as she studied the inside of the shuttle. 'From what vessel did this escape shuttle escape?'

'We live on the Aderinsola. It's an exploration ship.'

Margo raised an eyebrow. 'The human scientific vessel? I've heard of it. That must make you a human?'

Ayla furrowed her brow, confused why Margo would ask such a question. 'Of course I'm a human.'

Margo fixed her eyes on Teddy. 'And how did you come to live with the humans?'

Teddy was still standing by Ayla's side, calmly taking in the developing situation. He glanced up to Ayla's face before looking at Margo. 'Meowarow,' he told the new girl.

It was Margo's turn to appear confused. 'Are you having issues with your vocal implant?'

'He doesn't have a vocal implant,' Ayla said. 'What are you talking about?'

Margo slowly nodded her head. 'So he's a traditionalist gongadim? You don't see many of them nowadays.'

'He's not a gongadim,' Ayla insisted. 'He's a cat.'

Margo began to laugh until she realised Ayla was being serious. 'Okay. I'll take your word for it.'

More faces began to pop out from the smoke, making Ayla take a few steps backwards.

Margo noticed Ayla's movement and turned to see what was disturbing her. 'Ah, my crew have come to say hello,' she said. 'A nosey bunch, but the best crew a captain could ask for. Come and meet our guests everyone.'

The first crew member entered and Margo gestured for him to step forwards, a tall thin boy with scruffy brown hair. 'This is James,' Margo said. 'He's our chief engineer.'

A brown haired girl wearing glasses was next. 'This is Harriet. She's our chief medical officer.'

Next was a boy, his dark hair bouncing as he walked. 'Seb, he's our chief science officer.'

Two similar looking girls walked in, one slightly shorter than the other. 'Matilda and Meredith. Our very excellent pilots.'

A mass of curly hair on top of a small boy stepped into the shuttle. 'This is Dylan,' Margo said. 'Our chief comms officer.'

Two boys tried to walk through the open door side by side, but got stuck when their shoulders budged up against each other. A shove from someone behind forced them into the shuttle. They were both covered in grease and oil. Margo stepped to one side, giving them some room. 'Alex and Finley,' she said, 'our very messy mechanics.'

The boy who had shoved the mechanics stepped inside, swiftly followed by a much smaller girl. The boy was a giant of a child, but probably only ten years old. 'This is Charlie, one of our security officers.'

'Hey Cappy,' the girl behind Charlie said. 'Are you blind or something? What about me?'

Margo leaned to one side to look around Charlie. 'Sorry Bronte, I didn't see you there. This is Bronte, our other security officer. Don't let her size fool you. She can handle herself just as well as Charlie.'

They were almost fighting for places in the small shuttle, but still they continued. Next in was a confident little girl. She marched in and took her place in front of the rest of the crew, elbowing Charlie and James out of the way so she could get a good look at the newcomers. She smiled and nodded at Ayla. 'This is Emily,' Margo said. 'She's our navigator. We'd be lost without her.'

A few moments of silence passed. Margo was the first to turn and look at the doorway. It didn't take long for the rest of the Santacruise crew to do the same.

'Has anyone seen Izzy?' Margo asked.

'I'm here,' a loud voice announced from within the smoke. A small girl emerged and trotted inside. 'You left the ship in active mode, Captain,' she said with a scowl. 'It's dangerous if there's nobody on board.'

Margo smiled and turned back to Ayla, before rolling her eyes. 'This is Izzy, the ship's executive officer, and my biggest critic.'

'Call me XO,' Izzy told Ayla.

'How old are you all?' Ayla asked. 'Where are the adults?'

'I'm the oldest,' Margo replied, prodding a thumb at her own chest. 'I'm twelve, and Izzy is the youngest at six. Everyone else's ages vary in between.'

'Where are the adults then?' Ayla asked. 'Your parents, where are they?'

'You humans do things differently to us,' Margo explained. 'We aren't tethered to our parents like you.'

'But . . .' Ayla hesitated, puzzled by Margo's mention of humans again. 'Are you not humans?'

The whole crew guffawed with laughter, the noise filling the tiny cabin of the shuttle.

'HA HA!!!'
'HE HE HEEEEEE!'
'HOO HO HOOOOO HO HUMANS!'
'HA HA HA!'

'Do you honestly think we look like humans?' Margo asked, once the laughter had died down.

Ayla studied their very human-like faces, with their very human-like eyes, and noses, and ears, and mouths. 'Well yes, you do,' she replied.

'We're obviously enteenaps,' Margo said with a big grin. 'We don't have humans in the Triangulum Galaxy, unless you come here from your galaxy of course.'

'Which they do do a lot nowadays,' Harriet added.

'Hey Harriet,' Dylan laughed, 'you did a doo-doo.'

'Very funny, Dylan,' Harriet sarcastically said.

'Enteenaps?' Ayla breathed. 'I've never heard of enteenaps.'

'That's strange,' Margo said with a frown. 'Maybe the other humans on your ship aren't aware of our existence yet.' She pointed past her crew towards the red smoke. 'Anyway, please come on board our ship and eat something with us. We won't jettison your escape shuttle, so it will be close if your parents come looking for it. I'm sure Teddy would like something to eat.'

'I've never spoken to a gongadim before,' Izzy said, as she stared longingly at Teddy.

'Ayla claims he's not a gongadim,' James told her. 'She said he's a . . .' He paused and looked to Ayla. 'What did you call him?'

'He's a cat,' Ayla replied defensively.

'Certainly looks like a gongadim to me,' the burly Charlie added.

'And me,' Bronte agreed.

'And me,' Seb said. 'Harriet, what's your medical opinion?'

Harriet studied Teddy over her glasses. 'I can guarantee that is one hundred percent gongadim.'

'I'm sorry but you're all incorrect,' Ayla told them, crouching down to hug Teddy. 'This is my cat.'

'Come on everyone,' Margo said. 'These are our guests. If Ayla says Teddy is a cat, he's a cat. Enteenaps don't offend their guests.'

'Fair enough,' Charlie said. 'He's a cat.' He turned to Bronte and winked, obviously not believing a word the human was saying.

Ayla looked down at Teddy's emerald eyes. She was really hungry, so guessed her cat was as well. 'Okay,' she finally said, looking to Margo. 'Thank you for your kind offer. We'll come and eat something. Just promise me you won't lock us up and destroy our shuttle.'

Margo began to chuckle, but had to stop herself again when she realised Ayla was still being serious. 'I promise you we won't do that. We'd never do anything like that.'

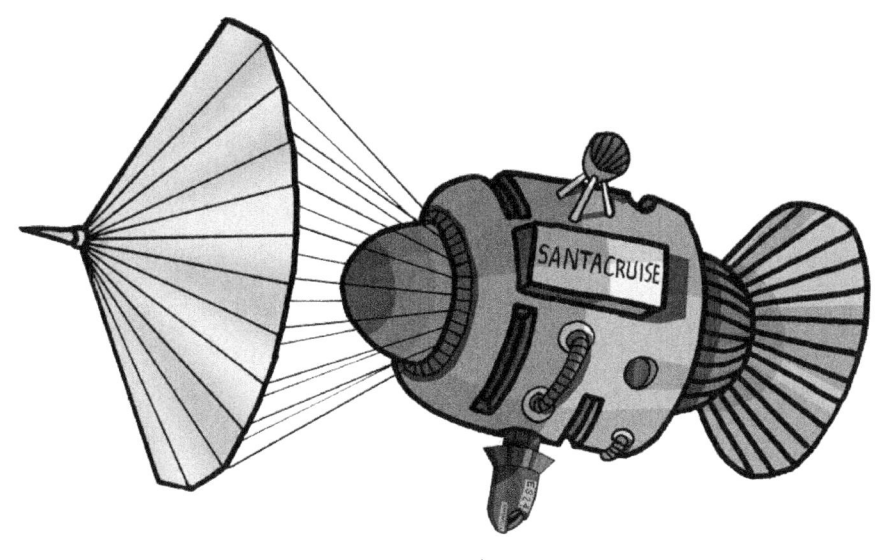

SPACE FOR A CAT

CHAPTER NINE

BOFFLE BALL

J N WOOD

The red smoke inside Margo's ship turned out to be steam leaking from coolant pipe outside the docking bay. Alex and Finley, the ship's mechanics, had been trying to fix it when they'd discovered Ayla and Teddy's escape shuttle. The steam was red because the docking bay's lights turned red whenever it was connecting to another vessel. Margo had explained this to Ayla as she hesitantly stepped into the steam, worried what was on the other side.

Teddy walked at her side as the crew guided them further into the Santacruise. The cat seemed to be taking everything in, but also kept one eye on the XO, Izzy. The little girl kept trying to get a closer look at him, forcing the cat to use Ayla as a barrier. Izzy seemed to be trying to get a closer look at the underside of Teddy's throat, and Ayla thought it was really freaking him out.

The ship's interior was similar to the Aderinsola, but the corridors were not as wide, and zero effort had been put into making it child-friendly. It was all sharp corners and hard surfaces. One huge difference between the two ships was the colours. Each and every wall in the Santacruise seemed to have been painted a different colour. Ayla hadn't realised there were so many colours.

'What kind of propulsion does your human ship use?' James, the chief engineer, asked her.

'I'm sorry but I don't know,' Ayla replied.

'How long did it take to fly here from the Milky Way Galaxy?' Seb, the chief science officer, asked.

'I was only a baby then, but I think it was about two years,' Ayla answered. 'I'm not sure though.'

'Your ship must have had faster than light capabilities then?' James asked.

Ayla shrugged. 'Maybe.'

'That's enough technical questions,' Margo said. 'We wouldn't divulge any of the Santacruise's secrets.'

'It's not that,' Ayla told them. 'I honestly don't know the answers. It might sound a bit daft telling you this, but I'm only a kid, and most kids don't know that kind of stuff.'

'Humans are weird,' James said.

'James,' Margo said, raising her voice slightly. 'Do not insult our guest like that.'

James's whole body had stiffened upon hearing his captain's voice. His back was straight and he was almost standing to attention. 'Sorry, Captain, and I'm sorry, Ayla. I didn't mean any disrespect. I only meant that humans are different to us. I never meant that Ayla was weird.'

'It's okay,' Ayla said. 'Humans can be pretty weird.'

'So why doesn't Teddy speak?' Izzy asked.

'He does speak,' Ayla replied, 'just not in our language.'

'Why don't you get James to take a look at his vocal implant,' Izzy suggested.

'Ayla has already told us he doesn't have one,' Margo told her.

'Well I didn't hear that,' Izzy said. 'Somebody had to make sure the ship was in the right mode while the entire crew was off organising a welcome party. I'm surprised there weren't balloons.' She turned back to Ayla. 'Why doesn't Teddy have a vocal implant? Is he one of those traditional types?'

'Cats don't have vocal implants,' Ayla said. 'I'd never even heard of vocal implants before today.'

'Oh yes of course,' Izzy said with a grin. 'I forgot that Teddy is a cat.'

'I bet if we check for an implant it'll be there,' Alex said. 'A quick scan will pick it up.'

'Nobody is scanning my cat for anything,' Ayla said.

'Don't worry,' Margo told her. 'Nobody is doing anything they don't want to.'

They entered a large room at the end of the corridor. Ayla thought it looked like a much bigger, and much more colourful, version of her family cabin on the Aderinsola.

'This is our communal living area,' Margo announced. 'Make yourself comfortable while we make dinner.'

'HEY AYLA!' Matilda shouted from the middle of the room. 'DO YOU AND TEDDY WANT TO PLAY BOFFLE BALL WITH MEREDITH AND ME?'

Ayla looked at the back of Margo as she made her way towards the kitchen, before turning back to Matilda. 'WE DON'T KNOW HOW TO PLAY!' she shouted.

'WE CAN TEACH YOU!' Meredith yelled as she placed a large boot on her foot.

'Do you want to play?' Ayla asked Teddy, but the cat was already walking towards the two girls. 'I guess you do.'

As Ayla approached them, Matilda threw her a pair of big grey boots. She expected them to be heavy, so flinched when she saw them flying through the air towards her. When she caught them she was surprised to find they weighed next to nothing.

'Put them on,' Matilda instructed as she started searching through a metal container. 'I know we've got two gongadim pairs in here somewhere. They should fit Teddy's paws perfectly.' She stood up straight, brandishing four identical boots to the ones Ayla held, but half their size. **'FOUND THEM!'** she jubilantly yelled.

Ayla kicked off her own boots and slipped her feet into the strange, oversized footwear. 'What are these for?' she asked.

'You can't play boffle ball without them,' Meredith replied. 'They create gravitational fields around your feet and legs so you can go wherever you want.'

Ayla had no idea what that meant, so she just nodded. Her expression must have given away what she was thinking, because Matilda felt like she had to explain. 'They stop the ship's artificial gravity from forcing you down to the floor,' she said. 'We play on the ceiling so we're out of everyone's way, otherwise Cappy Margo won't let us play at all. She reckons the game is too disruptive otherwise.'

SPACE FOR A CAT

CHAPTER TEN

A LITTLE HELP

J N WOOD

Meredith soared past Ayla at speed, almost skimming across the metallic silver ceiling like she was on ice. She twice bounced the holographic ball onto the ceiling before throwing it to Matilda. With Ayla hot on her heels, Meredith then darted past Teddy, who it turned out was an excellent boffle ball player, and received Matilda's perfectly angled pass. An instant later the ball slammed into Ayla and Teddy's target goal at the back of the room, making the score five to two in the pilots' favour.

'YOU'RE GETTING BETTER!' Matilda shouted. 'A FEW MORE GAMES AND YOU'LL BE AS GOOD AS US, ESPECIALLY IF

YOU HAVE TEDDY ON YOUR SIDE!'

Ayla was out of breath, so she leaned forwards and placed her hands on her knees. It still felt strange being upside down, with the rest of the crew going about their business beneath them. **'THANK YOU MATILDA!'** she yelled back. **'I THINK YOU'RE JUST BEING KIND! I'M A LONG WAY OFF BEING AS GOOD AS YOU TWO!'**

Meredith stopped behind Ayla and Teddy. 'Matilda is right,' she said. 'That assist for Teddy's second strike was genius. Neither of us saw it coming.'

'How are you so good at this, Teddy?' Ayla asked him.

'Meowarow,' Teddy replied.

'Gongadims are renowned for their boffle ball skills,' Meredith said.

'Meredith,' Matilda warned, as she skidded to a halt behind her.

'Sorry,' Meredith said, sounding genuinely apologetic. 'Cats must be good at it as well.'

'DINNER IS SERVED!' Margo announced.

'Game over,' Matilda said. 'We'll have to schedule a rematch soon.'

'Yeah maybe,' Ayla told her, although she was hoping her parents would be here soon. These kids seemed like they were nice, but she desperately wanted to be with her mummy and daddy.

After Meredith had managed to spin her the right way up and guide her back down to the floor, Ayla removed the boffle boots and then helped Teddy remove his. She eyed the cat suspiciously, looking for a clue, something that might confirm if he was indeed a gongadim.

'AYLA AND TEDDY!' Harriet shouted. **'COME AND GRAB A SEAT! THERE WON'T BE ANY PANKA LEFT IF YOU TAKE MUCH LONGER!'**

Ayla searched for two available seats as they made their way to the crowded table. Two chairs skidded away from the rest, pushed out by Dylan, the comms officer. 'These two are free,' he offered.

Teddy took two long strides and leapt up onto one of the chairs. Dylan leaned back and dragged it towards the table. 'I think someone is hungry,' he said.

Ayla sat down next to Teddy, who was already devouring the contents of his plate. She wasn't sure what the food was, but didn't want to ask in case they thought she was being rude. There were three large cubes on her plate, one red, one brown and one yellow.

'It's panka boom-boom,' Dylan said after noticing her apprehension. 'The red is the sauce, the brown is the meat, artificial of course, and the yellow is the panka. It's really nice.' He pointed at Teddy's almost empty plate. 'As you can see.'

She looked around the table at the content faces as they all happily ate. If Teddy liked the food, she thought, it must be okay. She picked up her fork and sliced off a corner of all three cubes, and then scooped them up and placed the forkful in her mouth. The taste was out of this world. She turned to Dylan. 'I've never heard of panka boom-boom before, but this is the nicest thing I've ever tasted.'

Dylan nodded slowly. 'It's no oontullbootellbops, but it's pretty good.'

'I need to try oontull . . . boo . . .' she tried to say.

'Oontullbootellbops,' Dylan told her. 'I think it's on the menu for this week sometime.'

'HEY, AYLA!' a voice yelled over the hubbub of cheery chatter. Ayla leaned forwards and spotted Emily looking back at her. 'Where was your ship when you had to jump in that escape shuttle?' she asked.

It was time for Ayla to feel embarrassed by her lack of knowledge again. Her face flushed bright red as everyone's eyes seemed to bore into her. 'I'm sorry but I don't know.'

'I don't know where I am right now,' Finley said, obviously trying to make Ayla feel better.

'You're sat at the dining table,' Alex told him.

Finley lightly punched his friend on the arm. 'I meant the ship. I don't know where we are in the galaxy.'

'But you know which galaxy you're in?' Emily asked him.

'Ha ha, Emily,' Finley said. 'We can't all be super-duper intelligent navigators. I bet you couldn't fix a leaking coolant pipe.'

'Neither can you,' Izzy said. 'There's one still leaking coolant all over the docking bay.'

Finley and Alex shared a quick glance. 'Oh yeah,' Finley said. 'We better fix that after dinner.'

Alex swallowed a mouthful of his food. 'I forgot all about that. Why didn't you remind us, James?'

James waved his knife dismissively. 'It's not that important. It can wait until we've finished our chow. I'll come with you. All three of us will have it done in no time.'

'Do you know why you had to escape your ship?' Bronte asked Ayla.

Ayla could barely see Bronte behind her fellow security officer, Charlie. She grinned, happy she finally knew the answer. **'ASTEROIDS!'** she exclaimed. **'IT WAS AN ASTEROID STRIKE!'** Her grin faded away when she remembered what had happened. 'The asteroids damaged the Aderinsola and then some more came and hit our shuttle. Teddy did his best to fly us through but there were too many.'

'Hey, Cappy Margo,' Emily said. 'Do you think Ayla's ship was near that planet that exploded all those years ago?'

'That's at least five hundred thousand miles away,' Margo said. 'Maybe a million.'

'It's the only place I can think of that will have that many asteroids,' Emily told her. 'The rocks are still orbiting that large moon. Maybe Ayla's ship got too close.'

'Do you know how long you were flying before we found you?' Seb asked.

'I passed out because we were spinning so much,' Ayla replied.

'It's okay,' Seb said. 'With your permission, I'll check the shuttle's computer, and Teddy's permission of course. It should tell me everything I need to know.'

'Yes that would be brilliant,' Ayla said, before looking at Teddy. 'That's okay isn't it?'

Teddy looked at Seb and said, 'Meow meow.'

'I'm sorry, Teddy,' Seb said. 'I don't understand gongadim.' Seb suddenly dropped his fork onto the table. **'OWWWW!'** he yelled. 'Who just kicked me?' He reached down to rub his shin with a hand. His eyes met with Harriet, who was shaking her head. Quickly realising why Harriet had kicked him, but not why she'd done it so hard, Seb said, 'Sorry, I don't understand cat, not gongadim.'

Ayla looked down at Teddy, who stared back at her. 'Don't worry about it,' she said. 'I'm beginning to have my suspicions.'

'That's a good idea Seb,' Margo said. 'If you can pinpoint where Ayla's journey began, we might be able to figure out where the rest of her ship's escape shuttles went.'

'So you'll help us find my parents?' Ayla asked.

Margo smiled. 'Of course we will.'

'That's brilliant,' Ayla said. 'Thank you very much.'

'We only have a small window of time to help though I'm afraid,' she said. 'We're transporting some important cargo and have a very strict deadline. We should be able to drop you off at one of the human space stations.'

'Cappy,' Charlie and Bronte both said in unison.

'Don't worry,' Margo told the security officers. 'We won't leave the ship. I'm not stepping foot on one of those places ever again.'

'Why do you say that?' Ayla asked. 'What's wrong with them?'

'We had a little problem the last time we visited one,' Bronte told her.

'The adult humans tried to capture us,' Charlie explained. 'They kept going on about taking us back to our parents.'

'But you want to go back to your parents so you'll be fine,' Bronte said. 'We were lucky to all get out of there.'

'Not all of us did get out of there,' Alex said, holding up his left hand. Ayla hadn't noticed before, but the tip of his little finger was missing. He turned to Ayla and Teddy. 'Got it caught in a door while we were escaping. If I'd been a little bit slower . . .' He slowly shook his head.

'That would have been the end of my life as a mechanic,' Finley mockingly added.

Alex turned to him. 'Well it would have been.'

'I know,' Finley laughed, 'but I've heard that story a hundred times.'

'It's decided,' Margo announced. 'After dinner, we get Ayla back to her parents.'

CHAPTER ELEVEN

SMELLS OF FISH

Ayla's excitement was crushed when Seb reported back with his findings.

'The shuttle's computer must have been damaged when it was struck by the asteroid,' he said. 'There was absolutely no data on the location of the shuttle's point of origin. There was very little data on anything, and the computer was barely functioning. I'm amazed Teddy managed to get you this far.'

Ayla could feel her eyes beginning to fill with tears.

'It's not the end of the world,' Margo said. 'We can still take you to one of the human space stations. We'll just have to take a guess at which one is the right one.'

Ayla wiped the tears from her face while Teddy rubbed his body against her leg. 'What if my parents are not there?'

'Someone on the space station will know where they are,' Margo told her.

'How many space stations do humans have around here?' Ayla asked.

Margo looked to Seb for the answer. 'Three, maybe four,' Seb guessed. 'The ones I can think of are all a similar distance from where we think her ship was destroyed.'

'We might get lucky then,' Margo said. 'Let's go to the bridge and ask Emily to plot us a course.'

They left the escape shuttle and returned to the Santacruise, first going through the docking bay, which was now free of coolant steam.

'Will you have time to take me to more than one space station?' Ayla asked.

Margo looked pensive, like she was carefully considering her response. 'I'm sorry, but I don't think we'll be able to do that. To be honest, we probably don't have the time, but on top of that, the crew don't want to go back to one human station, let alone two or three. They only agreed to the one because they like you and Teddy.'

Ayla was disappointed but understood, and was grateful for the help they were giving her. 'That's fine,' she said.

Seb slung an arm over Ayla's shoulders. 'Hey, don't worry so much. I've got a good feeling about this. I reckon we'll pick the right one.'

Ayla stood with Teddy at the back of the Santacruise's bridge, feeling very much like a spare part. Every member of the bridge crew had their designated place.

Captain Margo sat on her captain's chair, positioned high up above everyone else so she could keep an eye on the proceedings. The two pilots, Matilda and Meredith, sat at the front, steering the ship. Ayla was stood between Seb and Emily. Chief Science Officer Seb was doing something on his computers. Ayla assumed it was something scientific. The screen in front of Emily was ginormous, the biggest Ayla had ever seen. It was almost the size of her bedroom wall on the Aderinsola. Emily was using both hands to plot their course around the many stars and planets in their way. On one side of the captain, but his chair was at floor level, was Dylan, the chief comms officer. It was his job to monitor the communication zipping through space. On the other side of the captain was the XO's chair, but it was empty. Izzy roamed the bridge, occasionally checking in with a crew member to check on their progress.

'Emily, do we have an estimated time of arrival on the human space station?' Margo asked.

'ETA to Space Station B One Nine Eighty Six is approximately fourteen minutes,' Emily replied.

'We've made good time then,' Margo said. 'Five hours, very good in fact. Well done M and M.'

'Thank you, Captain,' Matilda and Meredith both said.

'Dylan, contact the station please,' Margo requested. 'Audio only. We don't want them to see our faces. They'd just try to board the ship so they could take us all back to our parents.'

Dylan sent the station a message asking for a connection. A man's gruff voice instantly replied.

'STATION B ONE NINE EIGHTY SIX DOCKING MASTER NUMBER FOUR TO UNIDENTIFIED VESSEL. IDENTIFY YOURSELF AND STATE YOUR INTENTION.'

Margo lowered her voice, trying to sound older than her twelve years. 'This is Captain Margo of the Santacruise. We picked up a stray escape shuttle from the ship known as the Aderinsola. It was carrying two occupants, who are both safe and well. Do you know if any other members of the Aderinsola are on board your station?'

'DO YOU EXPECT ME TO KEEP A RECORD OF EVERY ARRIVAL ON THIS STATION? DO YOU HAVE ANY IDEA HOW MANY PEOPLE COME AND GO ON THIS GODFORSAKEN PLACE?'

Margo shifted uncomfortably in her chair. 'Well ... no I don't ...'

'STATE YOUR INTENTION!'

Margo was taken aback by the man's rudeness, but decided she should stay courteous. 'My intention is to place the escape shuttle's former occupants back into the shuttle and shove it in your direction. Will you be able to pick it up?'

'WHY CAN'T YOU DROP THE SHUTTLE'S OCCUPANTS OFF YOURSELF? THERE'S A PRETTY PENNY TO BE MADE FROM SALVAGING A HALF-DECENT ESCAPE SHUTTLE. WHAT'S THE MATTER WITH THIS ONE? THIS SMELLS A BIT FISHY TO ME.'

'I can assure you that nothing smells fishy,' Margo said. She muted the audio and turned to Ayla. 'What does it mean when something smells a bit fishy?'

'A bit dodgy,' Ayla whispered.

'You can speak up,' Margo instructed. 'He can't hear you.'

'I think he's suggesting it sounds dodgy,' Ayla said.

Margo swivelled around and turned the audio back on. 'Nothing fishy at all, Sir. We merely have some time constraints. We've got some important cargo that needs delivering ASAP, so we don't have time for full docking procedures.'

'OKAY. PUSH THE SHUTTLE TOWARDS DOCKING BAY SEVENTY SIX. I'LL LIGHT IT UP FOR YOU SO YOU CAN SEE IT. WE'LL SEND THE CLAMPS OUT TO RETRIEVE IT.'

'Thank you very much,' Margo said. 'Give us fifteen minutes. Captain Margo out.'

'YEAH WHATEVER.'

'What a delightful chap,' Izzy said.

Ayla wasn't looking forward to entering this space station, not if the people on board were going to be like that guy. But if her parents were on board this scary place, it would be worth putting up with a few horrible people.

CHAPTER TWELVE

SANTACRUISE SALUTE

Ayla and Teddy stood in the entrance to their shuttle, while the entire crew of the Santacruise faced them in a line.

'When you enter the station you'll no doubt speak to one of the docking masters,' Margo told her. 'Ask them who you should speak to about finding your parents. They'll point you in the right direction.'

'We're really sorry we can't come with you,' Charlie said, 'but we can't risk getting rounded up and shipped off to some random human parents.'

Alex lifted the finger missing the end. 'Or risk losing more body parts.'

'That's okay,' Ayla said. 'I understand.'

'We haven't forgotten about that rematch,' Meredith said.

'Merowmeyumerow,' Teddy said.

'I think he said he hasn't either,' Ayla said with a smile.

'SANTACRUISE CREW!' Margo suddenly announced, the words making everyone stand to attention. 'Let's give Ayla and Teddy a proper Santacruise farewell.'

Ayla's dad always used the word farewell when saying goodbye. The memory of him saying it made her eyes glisten.

James raised his hand. 'Before we start,' he quickly said, 'the official Santacruise salute has changed so many times, I can't remember which version is the most recent one.'

'I think it's the one with the jazz hands and the big sweeping wave at the end,' Harriet said.

'No that was from ages ago,' Finley said. 'I thought it was the one where you high five the person next to you halfway through.'

'That was the first one we ever tried,' Bronte scoffed.

They all started suggesting the ones they thought were correct, shouting over each other while Ayla quietly chuckled. She would miss this very peculiar group of kids.

'OKAY! OKAY!' Margo yelled, quietening her boisterous crew. 'Just do whichever one you remember. Hopefully they'll match up.'

Ayla wasn't sure where to look when they started. Not one of them was in time with each other, or even close to doing the same routine.

At one point during the bizarre spectacle, James was doing a backflip . . .

Alex was on his knees with his t-shirt up over his head . . .

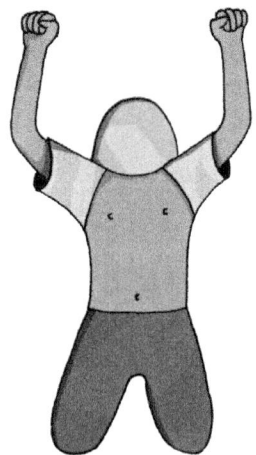

Harriet was hopping on one foot . . .

Margo was doing a double-handed, military style salute...

Bronte was sitting on Charlie's shoulders...

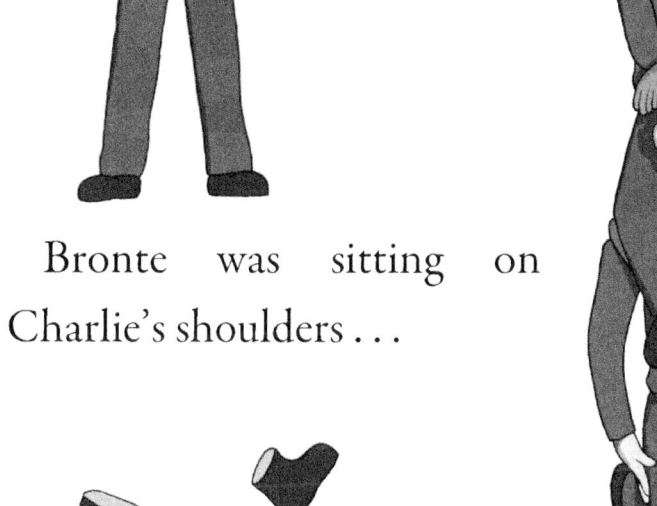

Seb was juggling with his own shoes...

Matilda and Meredith were sitting on the floor, pretending they were rowing a boat . . .

Finley was crouching down and flapping his arms like a bird . . .

Dylan was spinning around in circles on his head...

Emily was kicking her legs high into the air...

Meanwhile, Izzy was watching everyone else in utter disbelief, disgusted that nobody was doing the correct Santacruise salute.

Ayla loudly applauded when they'd all finally finished, each one at a slightly different time.

'Well,' Margo said, sounding out of breath, 'I can honestly say that was a resounding failure.'

'I absolutely loved it,' Ayla told them. 'It was one of the best farewells I've ever received.' She went to each and every one of them, giving them a big hug in turn. When she reached Margo at the end of the line she stopped. 'Thank you very much for helping us.'

'It's been our absolute pleasure,' Margo said, and pulled Ayla in for a hug. She then wrapped her arms around Teddy and gave him a squeeze.

Ayla and Teddy walked back to the shuttle's entrance before turning to face everyone. After a long wave goodbye, they both turned and walked through the doorway.

SPACE FOR A CAT

CHAPTER THIRTEEN

MY OTHER FACE IS BEAUTIFUL

J N WOOD

'I hope Mummy and Daddy are on this space station,' Ayla said.

Teddy was sat on the chair next to hers again. He was reaching up so his paws were resting on one of the shuttle's displays.

The shuttle disconnected from the Santacruise and they were soon floating in space. It wasn't long before two loud clangs echoed through the shuttle. The space station's clamps had found them and latched on, pulling them towards docking bay 76.

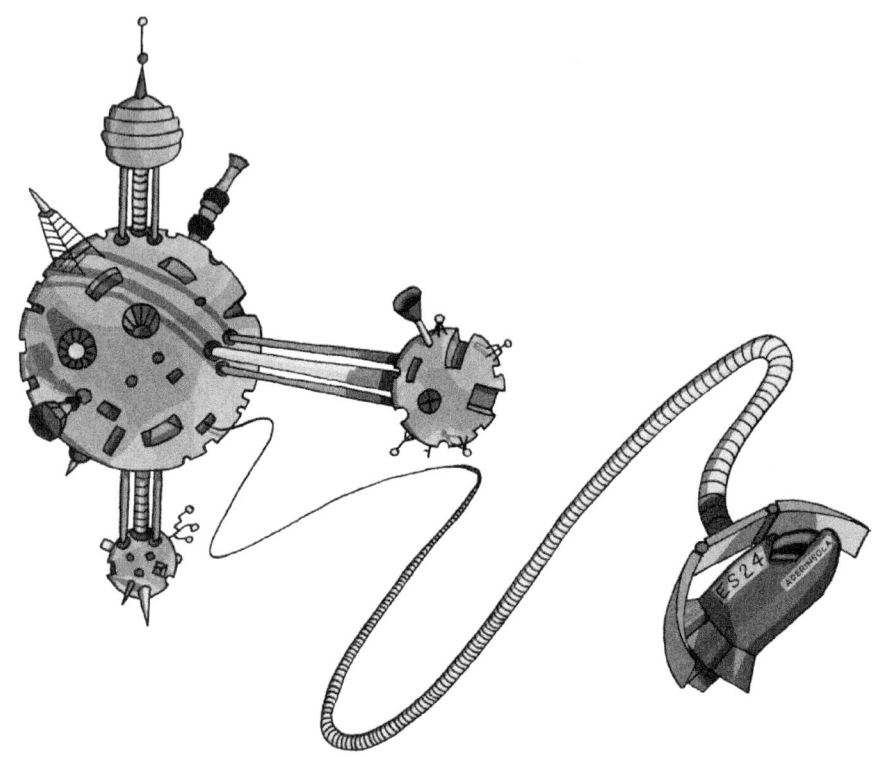

Ayla slipped off her chair and stepped towards Teddy, wrapping her arms around him and holding on tight. 'I'm nervous,' she whimpered.

Teddy nuzzled his face against the top of her head and purred loudly, the sound reverberating through Ayla's body, instantly calming her nerves.

'Thank you for being my best friend,' she said. 'Promise me you'll never leave me.'

A woman's voice made Ayla jump.

'SHUTTLE OCCUPANTS. PREPARE FOR DOCKING.'

'Please be here, Mummy and Daddy,' Ayla whispered.

The shuttle was jostled and bumped from side to side, up and down and back and forth, seemingly without a care for the safety of its occupants. Then they were still. Ayla expected the shuttle to tell them the airlocks were being opened, but today it was staying silent. She started walking towards the inner door with Teddy close by her side, when the door began to open.

A huge human shape leaned in and surveyed the scene. Interesting was the best word to describe the woman. She had a very bulbous and red nose, which only just drew the attention away from her flaky scalp. Ayla could see it was flaky because she had very little hair on her head, although there was plenty of hair protruding from her nostrils.

'I was told there were two of you,' the woman said.

'There are two of us,' Ayla insisted. 'Me and Teddy.'

The woman peered over her nose, studying the cat. 'Where are your parents?'

'I don't know,' Ayla said. 'We're trying to find them. We were hoping they might be on this space station.'

'What ship did this escape shuttle come from?' the woman asked.

'It was called Aderinsola.'

The woman slowly nodded her head, as if pondering a very complicated task. She stepped back so she was outside the shuttle. 'Come on out then,' she said. 'We better get you to security. They might know the whereabouts of your parents.'

Ayla looked down at Teddy, who had a worried expression on his face. 'We don't have much choice, Teddy,' she whispered, before following the woman.

From a platform high above docking bay 76, Ayla could see it was a vast, cavernous room. A huge amount of tents and market stalls spread out as far as the dark shadows would allow her to see. The walkways were bustling with people, and the air above them was jam-packed with hovering drones. The flying machines carried metal crates of all sizes, whizzing over everyone's heads.

Once they were down amongst the many market stalls, Ayla was mesmerised by the different smells and sights, but mostly by the unusual looking people as they streamed past. She needed to pay more attention to where she was walking, because she kept standing on the heels of the bulbous nosed woman leading them.

'Excuse me,' Ayla said, to no response from the woman. 'Excuse me Docking Master,' she said again, but a bit louder.

'I'm not the docking master,' the woman replied. 'I'm the trainee.'

'The ship I live on,' Ayla said, 'or the one I used to live on I suppose, it was damaged and everyone had to evacuate. Do you know if any of them came here?'

'I don't know,' the woman replied, 'but we're going to see the head of security. He'll know what to do with you.'

The woman took a sharp turn and entered a passageway lined with more market stalls, all selling food Ayla had never seen before. The only reason she knew it was food was because people were eating it. Otherwise she would have assumed the stalls were selling dirty clothes, because the smell was atrociously awful. She could almost feel the smell in the back of her throat, like it was trying to crawl further inside her.

The woman abruptly stopped, so suddenly that Ayla wasn't paying attention again and very nearly walked into her. If Teddy hadn't meowed, Ayla might have accidentally buried her face into the woman's large posterior. The hairy nosed woman slammed her clenched fist against a large metal door three times, the noise echoing around them.

BANG!!!
BANG!!!
BANG!!!

'**ENTER!**' a booming voice replied from the other side.

The woman opened the door and stepped inside, gesturing for Ayla to follow her.

'**SSSSLINK!!!**' the booming voice said. 'Long time no smell. What can I do for you?'

Ayla climbed the two steps. Inside was a large wooden desk but she couldn't see who the voice belonged to, the woman's large body obscuring the other person in the room.

'A stray came in on an escape shuttle,' the woman said. 'Claims to be from the Aderinsola, the exploration ship that blew up a few days ago.'

Ayla stepped to one side so she could see the man. He looked remarkably similar to the woman, their noses and physiques almost identical.

'Bring the stray here then,' the man said. 'I might be able to put it to some use.'

'She is here,' the woman said, and then spun around, trying to find where she'd left Ayla. 'Ah, here she is.' She grabbed Teddy by the scruff of his neck, and Ayla by the back of her t-shirt, lifting them both up off the floor.

Ayla kicked her legs and tried to reach back to get to the big woman's hands. **'HEY!'** she yelled. **'WHAT ARE YOU DOING?'**

'MEROWWWWWWWW!' Teddy yelled. All four of his paws were swiping at the woman's face, but she was holding him too far away, so he couldn't reach.

'What do you think of this little one then, Clink?' Slink asked.

'Very small,' Clink said approvingly, while slowly nodding his head and licking his lips.

'Excellent. The maintenance department always want them small. The smaller the better.'

'Yes I know, you imbecile,' Slink said. 'Why do you think I brought her here?'

'All right, all right,' Clink said, looking genuinely offended. 'There's no need for the insults. I don't call you bulging bum-bum nose anymore.'

'That's because I beat you into a bloody mess the last time you did,' Slink said, 'and I'm a lot bigger now. We're not kids anymore.'

'You'll always be my little sister,' Clink said, 'so just watch what you say to me.' He glanced down at Ayla and then back up to his sister. 'No chance of the small one's parents finding her then?'

Ayla was in a full-blown panic now. She didn't know what to do, or how to get out of this woman's grip. Teddy had his teeth bared, still trying to attack Slink's face.

'None of the Aderinsola shuttles landed here,' Slink replied, 'so it would be very unlikely for them to come here now.'

'They're looking for me,' Ayla said desperately. 'They'll come here to find me. I know they will.'

'Hand her over then and I'll take her down to see Blink,' Clink said, his hand outstretched towards Ayla. 'She'll love her.'

'What about the big cat?' Slink asked.

'What do you think?' Clink asked. 'Throw it outside. Better yet, sell it to one of the food stalls. Somebody will eat cat around here.'

'NOOOOOOOOOO!!!' Ayla screamed.

Clink leaned over, and keeping his distance from the fuming feline, took Ayla from his sister.

'TEDDY!!!' Ayla cried. **'LEAVE HIM ALONE YOU HORRIBLE WOMAN! GET YOUR HANDS OFF HIM!!!'**

Clink looked from Ayla to Teddy. 'Get that thing out of here,' he told Slink. 'It looks like it might scratch your eyes out if you're not careful.'

Slink opened the door and stepped outside, Teddy still held at arm's length from her face.

Ayla stretched her arms out and kicked her legs. **'PLEASE!'** she yelled. **'I'LL DO WHATEVER YOU WANT! JUST LET ME KEEP TEDDY!'**

Clink lifted Ayla so they were eye-level with each other. She could feel his hot, smelly breath on her face as he measured her up and down with his eyes. 'I think you'll fit perfectly,' he said. 'Let's hope you don't have a growth spurt anytime soon.'

The door swung open and Slink staggered inside. Blood dripped from her hand and her face was covered in scratches. **'IT GOT ME!'** she wailed. **'IT GOT MY BEAUTIFUL FACE!'**

Clink turned to his sister and smiled. 'Either you're incredibly deluded, or you have another face somewhere that I don't know about.'

Slink fell forwards so she lay on top of Clink's desk. She reached down and started opening the draws, searching through each one. **'DO YOU HAVE ANY BANDAGES? QUICKLY, I NEED TO SAVE MY FACE!'**

'There's a first aid kit in the third draw down,' Clink replied. 'Did you sell the cat to one of the stalls?'

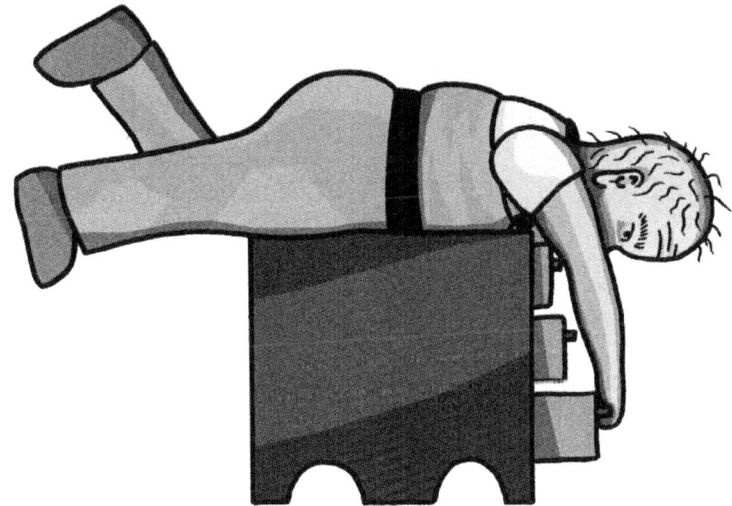

Slink stood up with the first aid kit in her hand. She pointed to her bloody chin with the red soaked hand. 'Are you being serious? It clawed me half to death before running away.'

Clink waved his hand dismissively. 'It hardly touched you,' he scoffed.

Ayla let out a little sob of relief, now she knew Teddy wasn't going to be sold for human consumption. Then it suddenly dawned on her how much trouble she was in, and she started to loudly weep. She was very much alone now.

'It's okay, little girl,' Slink said. 'I'll be okay once I'm patched up.'

'I WANT MY MUMMY AND DADDY!' Ayla cried.

'You'll soon forget about them,' Clink told her.

SPACE FOR A CAT

CHAPTER FOURTEEN

CABBAGE LEAVES

J N WOOD

Clink carried Ayla through the busy markets. She tried crying out for someone to help her, telling everyone she saw that she'd been kidnapped, but nobody listened. They barely gave her a second glance. Clink didn't even tell her to be quiet.

She constantly sought out Teddy, hoping to catch a glimpse of him hiding in the shadows, but there was no sight of him. She just hoped he was okay.

They left the markets and Clink started down a staircase. On and on he went, the stairs seeming to go on for ever. Ayla was worried they'd soon leave the space station and start floating through space.

By the time Clink unceremoniously plonked her down on a chair, in a rusty walled and damp smelling room, she was bereft of all hope. She had no idea where she was, and assumed they were so far from other people she would never find anyone to help her. She looked around at the brown and orange rust streaked walls, trying to figure out how things had turned so horrible, and so quickly.

'Hey, Clinkers,' a voice said. 'What brings you down to my neck of the woods?'

'Blink,' Clink said. 'I think it's kind of obvious.'

Another giant of a woman wearing a dressing gown stepped in front of Ayla. For a moment she thought it was Slink, but this woman was even bigger, with a lot more hair on her head.

'Well yeah,' Blink said. 'I noticed the little one, but you know me, I'm not one to assume anything.'

'Assume away, big sister,' Clink said. 'She's all yours. I thought she'd be perfect for your electrical piping jobs.'

Blink crouched down so she could properly examine Ayla. 'I think you thought correctly. That's not like you, Clink. Where did you find her?'

'I . . . erm . . . just found her in the markets, just wandering around and stuff.'

Blink looked up to her brother, one eyebrow cocked. 'You just found her in the markets? How can I be sure someone ain't gonna come looking for her?'

'I just know,' Clink said. 'You can trust me.'

Blink stood up straight and stepped closer to Clink. Her extra few inches in height meant she looked down at her younger brother's cowering face. 'Tell me the truth, otherwise I'll make your nose swell up so much you'll be able to tell people your massive hooter is a space station and charge them rent for living on it.'

Clink opened his mouth to say something but thought better of it. He tried again but just sighed. 'An escape shuttle landed at Slink's docking bay today,' he eventually said. 'This little one was the only person on board. Nobody is looking for her.'

'So it's Slink I need to thank,' Blink said, before stepping away from her brother and crouching down in front of Ayla again. 'You're gonna be good for me, Little One, very good.'

'My mummy and daddy are looking for me,' Ayla told her.

Blink looked at her brother. 'My mummy and daddy,' she said. 'How cute is that?' She turned back to Ayla. 'You don't have a mummy and daddy no more,' she growled. 'All you have now is me.' She took a large intake of breath and shouted right into Ayla's face.

'CABBAGE!!!'

'And you also have Cabbage,' she added. 'She will be your new best friend. I'm sure you'll get along like a house on fire.'

A tiny old woman waddled into the room. She was smaller than Ayla, with a wizened, almost skeletal face, topped by limp hanging, bright white hair. Ayla thought her skin looked like an artificial leather sofa her parents had once owned. Her mum had taken it down to the disposal units without her dad's knowledge, saying it was long past its expiration date. The faux leather had faded to a grey colour and started to crack.

'Yes, Blink,' the decrepit old woman said.

'Cabbage, Cabbage, Cabbage,' Blink said. 'I think this must be all of your birthdays and Christmas's rolled into one. I've found your replacement.'

Cabbage scowled at Ayla. Beneath the scowl was a glare fuelled by hatred. 'What does that mean for me?' she croaked. 'Do you not need me no more?'

Blink ruffled Cabbage's thin white hair, leaving her hand on the top of the old woman's head and using her as a leaning post. 'I still need you, my stinky Cabbage. Your new job is to train the new recruit.'

'So I don't need to crawl through the piping no more?' Cabbage asked.

'That's what I just said,' Blink replied. 'This little one is your replacement.'

Cabbage twisted her head around under the heavy weight of Blink's hand. She looked up to her master, her mouth contorted into something resembling a smile. 'Thank you, Blink. That's very good news. When does she start?'

Blink pushed off from Cabbage, almost shoving the old woman to the floor. 'No time like the present,' Blink said. 'Take her down to your hovel of a workshop and show her the ropes. We might as well get her into the pipes this afternoon.'

A look of bewilderment flashed across Cabbage's leathery face. 'But Blink, I ain't got no rope in my workshop.'

Blink shook her head. 'Just show her what we do here,' she told the old woman. 'One hour and the little one is in the pipes.'

'Mrs Blink,' Ayla said.

'Mrs Blink,' Blink said with a smile. 'Now that's what you call respect, Cabbage. You should take a leaf out of this little one's book.'

'Cabbage leaves,' Clink chuckled.

Blink laughed along with her brother. 'That's quite funny for you, Clink,' she said. 'Anyway, what do you want, Little One?'

'I don't want to go into the pipes,' Ayla pleaded. 'I just want to get my cat and find my parents.'

Blink grabbed Ayla under her arms and lifted her up so they were face to face. 'Get this into your tiny brain. You no longer have a cat or parents. You have nothing but me and Cabbage, although by the state of her, I doubt you'll have Cabbage for much longer.' She pulled her closer so the woman's big nose was pressed against Ayla's. 'Do you understand me?' she hissed.

Tears were freely running down Ayla's rosy cheeks. 'I don't know why I'm here,' she whined.

Clink dropped Ayla at Cabbage's feet. 'You'll know soon enough,' she told her. 'Cabbage, get her ready for the pipes. One hour and she's going inside.'

CHAPTER FIFTEEN

UNHAPPY FOLKS

Cabbage took Ayla into a room beneath Blink's office. There was only one working lamp in the corner, so it was very dimly lit. On the wall above the lamp was the room's only window. It was high up near the ceiling, with bars covering the glass.

Cabbage sat down on a very dirty mattress against a wall. She was surrounded by electrical components and reels of cable, so many reels it would have taken Ayla days to count them.

'This is your home now,' Cabbage told her. 'If you make it through the first year, Blink might get you a mattress to sleep on. You can make some room on the floor for now.'

'How long have you been here?' Ayla asked.

Cabbage looked up and blew a few white strands of hair from her cracked face. 'I'm guessing it's been seven years. Blink brought me down here when I was ninety years old, and I'm ninety seven now, so yes, seven years it is.'

Ayla was absolutely terrified. She'd never felt fear like it. 'I can't stay here for seven years,' she whispered. 'Mummy and Daddy will think I've gone forever.'

'You won't be here for that long,' Cabbage said. 'You'll grow bigger and Blink will dispose of you when she doesn't need you.'

Ayla clamped her eyes shut and willed her body to grow, to stretch beyond the height Blink needed her to be.

'What are you doing?' Cabbage asked. 'Don't poo your pants. There's a bucket over there.'

Ayla opened her eyes and was distraught to find she was still the same height.

'If you're not gonna have a poo, I'll tell you what your new job is,' Cabbage said, before throwing Ayla a belt covered in pouches and loops. 'This is your tool belt. I'll give you your tools just before you go into the pipe.'

'I've never done anything like this before,' Ayla complained. 'I don't know what to do.'

'It's easy,' Cabbage told her. 'You crawl through the pipes until you find any wiring chewed through by rats.'

'But I don't like rats,' Ayla said.

'Nobody here likes the rats,' Cabbage said, 'but you get used to them. It's your job to reconnect the wiring. We gotta keep the power going for the folks upstairs.'

Over the next hour, Cabbage gave Ayla a crash course on basic electrics. By the end of the lesson, Ayla felt like she knew even less about connecting electrical wiring.

'IT'S TIME, CABBAGE!' Blink's voice bellowed. **'GET HER INTO THE PIPES! THERE'S WORK TO BE DONE!'**

'What happens if I don't do it right?' Ayla asked the little old woman.

'The folks upstairs will be unhappy, which means Blink will be very, very unhappy. For your sake and mine, just make sure you do it right.'

SPACE FOR A CAT

CHAPTER SIXTEEN

NO RAT STEW FOR YOU

J N WOOD

Cabbage pointed to a tiny opening in a rusty metal pipe, attached to the ceiling by a series of metal brackets. The opening had to be tiny because the pipe was also tiny. 'You go in through there,' she said. 'I'm going to place a panel over the opening once you're in, so the only way you're getting out is to crawl two or three miles. I'll wait for you at the other end.'

'I don't think I'll fit in there,' Ayla said, staring at the opening. 'It's far too small.'

'I can fit in,' Cabbage told her, 'so you can too.' She leaned a ladder against the pipe before pointing to the heavily laden tool belt around Ayla's waist. 'You've got everything you need. It's probably best to keep an insulated screwdriver and the pliers in your hands. Sometimes the pipe is too tight to get the tools from your belt.'

'What if I get stuck?' Ayla asked. 'I'm bigger than you.'

Cabbage did a little shimmy and a shake with her whole body, a few of her old bones loudly cracking and popping. 'Just wriggle your way out,' she said. 'Now get on up there before Blink comes down here. It'll be much less painful for you if you go up there using your own hands and feet.'

Ayla searched her tool belt for the insulated screwdriver, and then found the little pliers that doubled up as wire strippers. She tentatively placed one foot on the bottom rung of the ladders and paused, before looking back to Cabbage. 'Why don't you just let me go? You can tell Blink I escaped or something.'

'Not a chance,' Cabbage replied. 'Get in the pipe.'

Holding back the tears, Ayla started to awkwardly climb the ladder.

'If you see a rat,' Cabbage added, 'kill it with the screwdriver. Make sure you take the dead ones with you to the other end and we'll eat them for dinner this evening.'

Ayla reached the top of the ladder and let out a shuddering sob. She didn't think she was still going to be alive by the evening. She peered into the dark interior of the pipe. 'I . . . can't . . .

see . . . anything,' she said between shoulder shaking sobs.

'This section isn't lit up,' Cabbage explained. 'But other sections will be. Just keep crawling until you can see something.'

'What if I don't find another light?' Ayla whined. 'Somebody might have turned them all off.'

Cabbage sighed and shook her head. 'Nobody has turned the pipe lights off. I'd suggest getting inside this pipe within the next ten seconds. Otherwise Blink will forcibly stuff you in there. You should probably stop crying. Wet tears and electricity don't mix well.'

Ayla never wanted Blink to touch her ever again. She took a deep breath and wiped her eyes with her sleeve. She knew she was strong enough to do this. All she had to do was get today out of the way, and then she would figure out how to escape. She laid the tools down inside the pipe and pulled herself in. She twisted and breathed in, holding her breath so she could squeeze her body inside. She could already hear Cabbage's hands and feet on the metal ladders, ready to cover the opening behind Ayla and lock her in. She needed to get moving and find some light before Cabbage reached the top of the ladder. Otherwise it would soon get even darker.

Using her elbows and knees, with her bum and shoulders scraping across the inside of the pipe, she shuffled forwards as quickly as she could. Her body was already blocking most of the light from the opening, but then Cabbage sealed her in and it became pitch dark.

For a brief moment she thought there was somebody else with her, another girl trapped in there, but then she realised the whimpers were her own. She was so scared she hadn't realised the squeaky noises were coming from her own mouth.

Ayla could occasionally feel wires touching her face as she crawled, but she couldn't see them so didn't even think about trying to fix them. Cabbage had warned her about not touching any live wires, but the ghastly old woman hadn't mentioned it being so dark she wouldn't even be able to see the wires. She was expecting to be electrocuted any second. There was a small light up ahead, so she started shuffling more rapidly to escape the terrifying darkness.

Ayla thought about how disgusting it would be to eat rats, but then realised she might have to eat some in order to get herself out of this predicament. If she consumed enough of them, maybe she would be too fat to fit in the pipes, and Blink would let her go. As she approached the illuminated section up ahead, she saw one of the rodents. A furry creature was scurrying towards her with its head down, entirely unaware of Ayla's presence. She managed to lift the arm holding the screwdriver, poised to strike if the rat came too close.

But she couldn't do it. She'd never harmed another living thing in her life, and wasn't about to start now. She brought the screwdriver down onto the metal surface below her. A loud clang filled the pipe and the rat stopped. It lifted its head and looked at Ayla in the gloomy darkness.

The rat's nose lifted and sniffed the air for a moment, before it quickly turned around and ran back in the opposite direction. Ayla let out a sigh of relief. She didn't want to think about what might have happened if the rat had come straight towards her.

She continued with her slow approach towards the light, and could already see some wires that had been gnawed at. She assumed that rat was probably the culprit. When she reached the first frayed wires, she was surprised to find she knew how to fix them. She'd just needed to have them in front of her before Cabbage's instructions started to make sense. She got to work and was glad of something to take her mind off the feeling of claustrophobia, not to mention the fear of rats nibbling at her feet.

Ayla worked tirelessly over the next few hours, fixing everything that needed her attention as she made her way through. She only saw a few more rats in that time, but still couldn't bring herself to hurt them. Each time she had to thwack the screwdriver against the hard metal surrounding her, or shout a quick warning, and the rats would disappear into the darkness.

Ayla was wondering if the end of this nightmare would ever come, when Cabbage's head popped up in front of her.

'How many rats did you get?' Cabbage asked. 'I'm starving.'

'None,' Ayla instantly replied. 'I didn't see any.'

'NONE!' Cabbage cried. She shook her head and gave Ayla a very disappointed glare. 'Get out of the pipe. I hope you like water, because that's all we're having tonight.'

CHAPTER SEVENTEEN

MY HERO

J N WOOD

Cabbage dragged an exhausted Ayla into Blink's damp and smelly office.

'How did she do?' Blink asked Cabbage.

'She didn't get any,' Cabbage replied forlornly.

Blink slammed a large industrial battery down onto her desk, sending fractured pieces of plastic in all directions. **'SHE DIDN'T FIX ANY OF THE WIRING?'**

'No I think she fixed everything,' Cabbage said. 'She didn't get any rats.'

Blink laughed and threw what was left of the old battery to the floor. 'I'm sure you'll survive a night without your exquisite rat cuisine, Cabbage. Now get some sleep. The little one will have a full day in the pipes tomorrow. She'll definitely bring home the rats after that.'

If Ayla hadn't been so tired, she probably would have cried again, although she didn't think she had any tears left. Cabbage grabbed her elbow and pulled her towards the steps leading down to the workshop. Ayla followed but her feet dragged across the dirty floor.

'Get some rest,' Cabbage told her once they were downstairs. 'It'll be a busy day tomorrow. One thing to remember, the only way out of here is through Blink's office upstairs, so don't get any grand ideas of escaping.'

Ayla was too exhausted to think about anything other than sleep. She slowly spun around, looking for some room amongst the mess covering the floor.

Cabbage sat down on her mattress and opened a water container. 'Kick some stuff out of the way,' she told her.

Ayla tried kicking a reel of cable but it didn't budge. All the kick resulted in was a very painfully stubbed big toe. She gave up and collapsed on top of everything, immediately falling asleep, until Cabbage woke her up four seconds later.

'Hey, do you want some water?'

'No thank you,' Ayla murmured, before falling asleep again.

The next time Ayla woke up it was the middle of the night. She could hear something, a fizzing noise of some sort. She could also feel something hitting her legs, not as heavy as water but quite warm. She sat up with a start, thinking Cabbage might have been weeing on her.

Orange glowing sparks were falling through the air and bouncing off her legs, eventually fizzling down to nothing. She followed the sparks' trajectory to see they were coming from the window near the ceiling. The orange glow suddenly ended, and the last of the burning embers floated down towards her.

There were no more bars in the window, and the glass that had once been behind them was no longer there. Teddy's face appeared in the opening.

'**TED . . .**' she began to shout, before clamping a hand over her mouth. She looked over to Cabbage, still curled up on her mattress. The little old woman seemed to stir from sleep slightly, but soon resumed her light snoring.

'Meow,' Teddy whispered.

Ayla slowly got to her feet, being extra careful not to make any more loud noises. She looked up to Teddy, instantly realising there was no way she could reach him without ladders. She hadn't seen where Cabbage had stored the set they'd used to reach the pipes, and didn't want to start searching through Blink's office. That would have probably meant finding the gigantic woman in the process.

Ayla remembered what was piled up beneath her feet, and knew what she needed to do. She picked up two of the heavy reels of cable and walked over to the wall under the window, where Teddy still looked down with concern. She stacked them on top of each other and looked around for some more. She didn't have to go far to find two more, and two more after that. She picked up reels after reels and stacked them up high, all the while trying to stay as quiet as a space mouse.

Ayla only needed three more reels before she could reach the window. She carefully crept back down the steps to collect them. She stacked three reels of cable in her hands and placed one foot on the first step. She couldn't see a thing with the reels in front of her face, so she was being very careful to place her feet in the right place with each step. She was very pleased with her stacking, as the hastily built stairs felt very secure and stable beneath her.

A loud rasping cough from Cabbage made Ayla freeze, right when she was about to place a foot on the fifth step. She balanced precariously, the third and fourth stacks wobbling slightly beneath her and almost making her drop the reels in her hands.

'Merow, merow,' Teddy whispered.

Ayla managed to turn and look down at Cabbage without losing her balance. The old woman rolled over, and Ayla was sure she'd been caught, but Cabbage's eyes were still closed, and she continued to roll until she was facing away from Ayla's newly created staircase. With a sigh of relief, Ayla turned to face Teddy and carried on.

Ayla's heart was in her mouth every time she placed all of her weight onto the next step, because they were now eight or nine reels high. There was a lot of movement going on beneath her, making her wobbly legs shake even more.

She was almost within touching distance of Teddy when the stacks behind her began to topple.

'MEROWROWROW!!!' Teddy yelled.

Ayla couldn't stop herself from risking a look behind. Cabbage was launching herself up the stairs like a woman half her age, no, more like a woman a quarter of her age. She was using the stairs with no concern for its stability, so reels were flying in all directions.

Ayla spun around and quickly placed the reels in her hands down on the last two steps. She ran up them and jumped up towards Teddy. Both of her hands grabbed the edge of the window and she pulled with all her strength, dragging herself upwards.

Bony fingers wrapped tightly around Ayla's right ankle, so firmly it immediately bruised her skin. She yelped in pain and tried to pull her leg from the old woman's death grip, but she couldn't escape.

'BLINK!!!' Cabbage screamed. **'THE LITTLE ONE IS TRYING TO ESCAPE! COME QUICKLY!!!'**

The sound of Blink crashing through her office was heard almost immediately, just as the stacks beneath Ayla began to collapse. Ayla thought her escape had definitely failed, and she would have to live in this horrible place forever.

Teddy jumped through the window and ran down Ayla's back, before launching himself at Cabbage's face. The old woman only caught a glimpse of the cat, but all she really saw was a flash of teeth and claws. She let go of Ayla and tried to protect her face with her hands. When they connected, Teddy and Cabbage fell to the floor, the cat clawing and biting the woman's leathery skin all the way down. Teddy thought she tasted a bit like that sofa Morrie and Kyra had once owned.

Unburdened by the death grip of the ninety-seven-year-old woman, Ayla managed to pull herself through the window, just as the last of the stacks fell to the floor. She immediately spun around and leaned into the room, trying to spot Teddy in the expanding cloud of dust.

'TEDDY!' she called out. **'WHERE ARE YOU?'**

A few reels were pushed aside as something started to emerge from beneath the chaos. The dust settled and Ayla's hopes of it being Teddy were dashed. The thing emerging from beneath the piles of reels was Cabbage.

'WHAT'S GOING ON DOWN THERE, CABBAGE?' Blink called out from upstairs.

'**THE LITTLE . . .**' The old woman stopped shouting and began to cough, spluttering even more dust into the air. '**THE . . .**' She had to stop again, this time bending over double and coughing up more dust. The rasping noise seemed like it would go on forever.

'**I'M COMING DOWN!**' Blink yelled.

'**TEDDY!**' Ayla cried.

The dirty, dust covered head of Ayla's cat appeared from beneath a large pile of reels. He was struggling to fight his way from under the heavy cables.

'**YOU CAN DO IT, TEDDY!**' Ayla yelled. '**COME ON!**'

With one final heave, Teddy was free, the tip of his tail the last part of him to emerge. He instantly started sprinting towards Cabbage, who was still bent over and heaving her guts up. He was going full speed, faster than Ayla had ever seen him run. In one swift motion, he leapt onto Cabbage's back and used her to propel himself towards Ayla and the window. He was moving through the air so quickly his ears were pinned back and his mouth was flapping open in the wind. Some of the dirt on his fur was dropping away to fall behind him. Ayla reached out as far as she could, hoping to catch Teddy if needed.

It wasn't needed.

The cat's trajectory through the air had been planned absolutely perfectly. He landed on Ayla's back, only just fitting through the small window.

He had, of course, made sure to retract all of his claws before hitting her. She rolled over and hugged him to her chest, just as Blink's voice filled the workshop beneath them.

'WHAT ON MARS ARE YOU DOING DOWN HERE, CABBAGE?' she screeched.

'Meowmerow,' Teddy said, before stepping off Ayla and moving away from her. He looked back after a couple of paces, wanting her to follow him.

Ayla tried standing up but cracked the top of her head into the ceiling. They were in a very low passageway, so Ayla had to bend her neck if she wanted to stand up straight. She trod on something hard and lifted her foot to see what was there. It looked like a laser cutter, similar to the one her dad owned. He used to constantly tell her she wasn't allowed to touch it.

Teddy started running and Ayla immediately followed. The cat ran at a pace he knew Ayla could manage, constantly looking back to check if she was okay.

Ayla knew they weren't free just yet, but she couldn't stop the smile creeping onto her face, even with a sore head and a bruised ankle. Her cat had saved her again. He was, and always would be Ayla's hero.

SPACE FOR A CAT

CHAPTER EIGHTEEN

THE RUBY

J N WOOD

Blink's shouts and screams followed them as they ran through the low passageway. Her voice sounded incredibly close, but also very far away at the same time. She was yelling all kinds of horrible things, the terrible acts she would perform on Ayla when she found her. She was threatening to rip the space station apart to get to her.

Ayla couldn't see a way out of this horrific situation. They were trapped on the space station. They couldn't go back to the escape shuttle because it didn't have any fuel. She wondered if she could contact the Santacruise somehow and ask Margo if she'd come back for them, but she didn't have any access to a communication hub. For the time being at least, Teddy seemed to have a destination in mind, constantly taking left and right turns, but Ayla didn't know if that was just a ploy to try and lose Blink and Cabbage. They couldn't live in the depths of this space station forever. They would no doubt outlive Cabbage, Blink, Clink and Slink, so they could hide down here and eat rats until the four evil people were gone. Ayla shuddered at the thought.

By the time they reached the end of one of the passageways, Blink's voice could still be heard, but it was at least faint. Ayla stopped alongside Teddy and dropped to her hands and knees. The cat was peering through a wire mesh panel. On the other side was a massive, open room, full of people and docked ships. It looked like docking bay 76.

'We can't go out there,' Ayla warned. 'What if Slink is working tonight?'

Teddy stopped licking the dirt from his fur and looked at Ayla, shaking his head.

'You know that Slink isn't working at the moment?' she asked him.

Teddy briskly shook his head once more.

'You don't know if Slink is working?' Ayla asked.

Teddy rolled his eyes before looking at the floor. He lifted his head again and slowly nodded his head.

'I'm sorry, Teddy. I don't understand.'

Teddy pushed the mesh panel with his nose, forcing it to swing outwards on two large hinges. He gently took one of Ayla's sleeves in his mouth and pulled her towards the edge. A metal ladder was attached to the wall, leading down to the floor.

'Are you sure this is where we need to go?' she asked.

Teddy stared her straight in the eyes and nodded his head.

'Okay, I trust you with my life.' She ducked down and waited for the cat to jump on her shoulders so she could take him down the ladder, but he just swung his back legs out first and started climbing down without her. Ayla watched him for a few seconds, amazed a cat could do that. He looked like a human. She did the same and swung her legs out until she felt a metal rung under her feet, and followed Teddy down.

Many drones flew past them, some of them pausing for a moment to inspect the cat and the child descending the long ladder. They both ignored the flying lumps of metal. Ayla was desperate to get her feet back onto something more solid, so didn't want any distractions.

That was when she realised that this couldn't be docking bay 76, the one where Slink worked, because that had been at the top of the space station, and they were still at the bottom somewhere. She felt a little bit safer with that knowledge, although she still couldn't be absolutely certain. She'd become a little disorientated following Teddy through the many passageways with low ceilings.

They finally reached the bottom of the ladder and Teddy instantly moved away, heading towards the throng of people milling around the many market stalls.

Ayla suddenly remembered all of the people who ignored her cries for help when Blink was carrying her. She felt sure one of them would instantly grab her and take her back to Blink.

Ayla stepped behind a large metal container. 'Teddy,' she called out. 'Wait.'

Teddy stopped and turned back to her, finding her face peering out from around a corner.

'What if one of these people works for Blink?' she asked.

Teddy shook his head and then looked back over his shoulder. He started pacing, like he was agitated about something. 'Merow, merow, merow, merow, merow.'

'Do we need to go that way?' Ayla asked.

He stopped and nodded his head.

'Okay, but stay close to me please.'

Teddy immediately stepped in front of her and turned to face the right way.

Ayla took a deep breath. 'I'm ready, Teddy. Let's go.'

They entered the gloom of the crowds, Teddy easily slipping between the many legs. Ayla didn't find it quite as easy so struggled to keep up with him at times, but he always stopped if he got too far ahead so she could catch him up. Ayla kept her head down and tried to avoid making eye contact with anyone, hoping they wouldn't notice her at all.

It felt like they'd been in the dark forever, enclosed by loud people on all sides, but then they were suddenly free and Ayla felt like she could breathe again. Teddy had waited for her to fully emerge from the mass of people, but now he was running.

'**MEROW, MEROW, MEROW, MEROW!**' he yelled back at her.

Ayla started running to try and catch him up. He seemed to be heading straight for a small ship that was readying to leave. Random bursts of steam and smoke splurged from underneath the hull, while orange and green lights on its surface flashed intermittently.

Teddy disappeared into a plume of expanding smoke, sending Ayla into a panic. **'TEDDY!'** she cried.

He instantly ran back to her, stopping at her side and nudging her legs, trying to hurry her along. They were soon climbing a ramp, but Ayla had no idea where it led, not being able to see anything but grey and white smoke.

'Where are we going?' she asked. 'Are we boarding a ship?'

'Meow,' Teddy replied.

'Ah Sefu,' a voice called out. 'We didn't think you were going to make it. Some of us had all but given up on you. Where is the young human you were speaking of?'

'Meowarow,' Teddy said.

Ayla looked for Teddy but she couldn't see him. She moved towards the sound of his voice while the ramp closed behind her. With a loud thud the ship was sealed and the smoke quickly started to disperse, eventually disappearing completely. Teddy was sat next to a black cat, maybe twice the size of him, and Ayla had always assumed Teddy was a big cat. She thought the black cat might have been one of those Earth creatures she'd seen in images, a panther maybe.

'There you are,' the giant cat said. 'Sefu has told us so much about you. Welcome aboard the Ruby. She is now your home for as long as you need her to be.'

Ayla was mesmerised by the cat's mouth. It was moving perfectly in time with the words he spoke. To say she was shocked would have been an understatement. She stood with her mouth agape, her eyes switching between Teddy and his new giant friend.

'My name is Kemnebi,' the black cat added. 'I'm the captain of this fine ship. I hope you're feeling better after your recent ordeal.'

Ayla continued to stare at him with disbelieving eyes.

Kemnebi frowned at the mute human, with concern in his bright orange eyes. He turned to Teddy. 'I think the gongadim's got her tongue. Is your human sister okay?'

'Meow meyuaru,' Teddy replied.

'Fair enough,' Kemnebi said. 'I suppose I was quite shocked when I first met an enteenap. We need to get you two secured before we launch, so follow me.' He turned and started padding away from them.

Teddy went to follow him but paused to look back at Ayla. She still looked astonished, with her feet frozen to the spot. 'Meow,' he quietly said. 'Merowmerow.'

Ayla managed to close her mouth and pointed in the direction Kemnebi had gone. She found that words were beyond her.

Teddy nodded and followed the captain, so Ayla followed Teddy. What else was there to do?

SPACE FOR A CAT

CHAPTER NINETEEN

MY NAME IS SEFU

J N WOOD

It wasn't easy, but Ayla and Teddy managed to catch up with Captain Kemnebi. The large animal's long, powerful legs moved him along at a fast pace. His fur was jet black and very glossy, like it had just been shampooed a few minutes ago. She thought he looked very strong, almost noble in the way he prowled through the ship.

The Ruby looked like any other ship, apart from having much lower ceilings. Ayla was fine with the ship's dimensions, but she thought her parents would have been constantly banging their heads. Blink, Clink and Slink would never have fit inside. She closed her eyes and silently thanked Teddy for saving her from those horrible people.

'Ayla,' Kemnebi said. He waited for her to open her eyes, before looking at the door next to them. 'This is your cabin. It's been converted to accommodate enteenap guests, so you should find it very comfortable. The whole crew has probably slept on the bed in there at some point. All of the chairs inside double up as safety seats. Pick one and strap yourself in.'

'What about Teddy?' Ayla asked.

Kemnebi smirked and looked at Teddy. 'He is going to come with me. He's asked us to take a quick look at his vocal implant. He should be back with you before we launch, but don't worry if he isn't. We'll take good care of him.'

'Merowaroo,' Teddy said, before poking his nose towards the door.

'So you are a gongadim then?' she asked her friend.

Teddy stared back at her, his emerald eyes glowing brighter than ever.

'Of course he is,' Kemnebi said. 'Now in you go. The humans have only given us a short launch window, so time is of the essence. Don't forget to strap in.'

She stepped to the door and pushed it open. It looked nice inside, a bit too white and grey coloured for Ayla's tastes, but nice enough. 'Okay. I'll see you soon, Teddy. Good luck with your vocal implant thingy.'

'Meow,' Teddy said, before he walked away with Kemnebi.

'Don't forget your safety belts, young lady,' Kemnebi said over his shoulder.

Ayla stepped inside the cabin, not sure what she should be thinking. If Teddy was a gongadim, he'd probably want to stay with other gongadims.

She very loudly sighed, not wanting to lose her best friend. She picked one of the four chairs around a table and pulled the two safety belts over her shoulders. If Teddy could talk now, he definitely wouldn't want to be someone's pet. He would be able to do anything he wanted. She took in the rest of the cabin. There was a large double-sized bed taking up most of one end, covered with a very comfortable looking duvet. It was very tempting to take off the safety belts and dive onto the bed. She could have easily snuggled up inside the duvet and slept for weeks. She hoped there weren't any complications when the other gongadims were fixing Teddy's vocal implant. She didn't want him to get hurt. On the other side of the cabin was a table and four chairs, one of which Ayla was sat on. Next to her was a sofa and a small table. She missed Teddy already.

'I'm back,' a deep voice said.

She spun around to find Teddy striding into the cabin.

'They fixed my implant,' he said. 'I didn't realise it would be that quick.' He jumped up onto the chair next to her and sat down.

She thought he looked exactly the same as always, with his big green eyes fixed on hers.

'I missed you when those big people took you away,' he told her. 'I didn't think I'd ever see you again.'

Ayla's eyes began to glisten when she couldn't contain her emotions any longer. She leaned over and pulled him in for a hug, soaking his shoulder with her tears. 'I love you, Teddy.'

'I love you too,' he said.

'Do you really?' she asked. 'Because you're not a cat, but we treated you like one.'

It felt to Ayla like her insides suddenly plummeted to the floor. Kemnebi's ship had left the ground and was beginning to exit the space station. She held onto Teddy as the safety belts dug into her shoulders.

'You treated me like your family,' Teddy said. 'Let me tell you the story of how a gongadim called Sefu became a cat named Teddy.'

SPACE FOR A CAT

CHAPTER TWENTY

SEFU'S TALE

J N WOOD

Seven years ago the Triangulum Galaxy was much the same as it is now. Humans had been visiting for a few years, gongadims and boomgaboons were well into the midst of their great war, and enteenap ships flew from planet to planet. The first human space station had recently been completed, going by the name, FK2347. It had been built on the route most human ships preferred to use on their journey to this galaxy.

Sefu was a pilot on board a gongadim battle ship called the Leopold. The vessel's purpose was to patrol the outer edges of the Gongadim Empire. The Leopold, along with its two sister ships, were there to act as a deterrent for the marauding boomgaboon ships.

On a day like any other, the Leopold responded to a distress call from a team of geologists on one of the gongadim's outlier moons. By the time the ship was in orbit around the moon, the distress call had stopped being transmitted. Sefu and three other crew members were tasked with flying a shuttle down to the surface. Upon arrival, they didn't find what they were expecting.

They had been lured into a trap, set up by the boomgaboons. The geologists didn't exist, at least not on this moon. The only living things on the surface were boomgaboons, who had stolen the identifications of a gongadim team of geologists from another moon. Sefu and his crew mates were taken hostage and flown back to the boomgaboon ship on the dark side of the moon.

Much later, Sefu found out that his captors had been attempting to exchange Sefu and his pals for several boomgaboons imprisoned on the gongadim home world, Azibo. At the time though, he had no idea what their plans had been. He was held in a tiny prison cell for months with no idea what was going on in the rest of the galaxy.

Early one morning, three months into his captivity, four boomgaboons marched into his cell and dragged him out into the corridor.

One of them was wearing magnified spectacles and inspecting Sefu's neck. A scalpel was soon in the bespectacled boomgaboon's mouth. Before Sefu could protest, the sharp blade was inserted into his throat, seriously damaging the vocal implant contained within.

Sefu recovered from his injuries but soon found himself in an even smaller cell. He was sold to a pet stall on the only human space station in the area, FK2347. The boomgaboons had promised the docking master's trainee a cut of the takings if he took the four gongadim prisoners to the market. The young lad told the stall holder the animals were exotic Earth cats, and could fetch her some decent money if she sold them.

Sefu spent five miserable weeks in that tiny cage, with only water and the odd scrap of food to sustain him. He could only sit and watch as his three friends were purchased by humans and taken away from him, never to be seen again.

Then one day, when Sefu was feeling at his lowest, two adult humans carrying a baby human stopped in front of his cage. The two adults took their time to study the malnourished animal, talking about how they were very concerned by his appearance. The baby just stared at Sefu's eyes, entirely engrossed in the shimmering green.

Sefu was genuinely distressed when the adults took the baby away. The exchange they'd shared had been the most meaningful thing to happen to him in months.

The adults very angrily approached the market stall holder, loudly asking her if she had a licence to sell exotic cats. An argument ensued, with the market stall holder claiming she didn't need a licence. The human couple didn't want to concede and threatened to report her to the station's security. The stall holder scoffed at this notion, telling them they'd struggle to find security, and would probably have more chance of finding a naturally growing tree. Heated words continued to be exchanged for many minutes, until the three adults reached a stalemate, with neither side willing to back down. After a brief moment of silence, the female human briskly shook her head and took some money from her bag. She leaned over the array of furry creatures and handed the money to the market stall holder, who grinned and nodded her head in response. The male adult did not look happy when he picked up Sefu's cage and carried the poor animal away. Sefu just hoped they were taking him somewhere quieter, somewhere he could sleep.

The humans eventually released him from his cramped confinement once they were inside their cabin. He felt so weak and tired, as it had been impossible to sleep in the bustling twenty-four-hour market, he collapsed on their sofa and instantly fell asleep.

Over the following weeks, with the humans' care and attention, he slowly regained his strength. Once he was stronger, he tried escaping his new home a number of times, but the humans always managed to prevent him from leaving, thinking it was just a game their cat was playing.

He found out that the adults were called Morrie and Kyra, and the baby was called Ayla. The humans obviously had no idea he was called Sefu, so they named him Ted, but as Ayla's grasp of language improved, she began calling him Teddy.

Sefu's outlook on his predicament changed when baby Ayla started to crawl and then walk. It was before she'd started affectionately calling him Teddy, but Sefu had a drastic change of heart. He realised he'd fallen in love with the child, probably from the moment their eyes had first locked onto one another in the market. He knew he had to stay because she needed him to keep her safe, but he also couldn't bear the thought of leaving her. He made it his sole purpose to protect his little human.

SPACE FOR A CAT

CHAPTER TWENTY ONE

LUXURY FUR

J N WOOD

Halfway through Teddy's story, Ayla had unclipped the safety belts and walked over to the bed. She had dived onto the duvet, savouring how utterly snuggly it felt. The luxurious and velvety feel was exactly what she'd hoped for. It was no wonder the gongadims sometimes slept here. Teddy had sat down next to her while she made herself comfortable and continued with his tale. By the time the story was over, Ayla was fast asleep with a big smile on her face. Teddy positioned himself behind her and closed his eyes, a feeling of contentment washing over him. It didn't take long before he joined Ayla in the land of nod.

Ayla woke up to find she was surrounded by cats, or gongadims. She told herself she had to stop calling them cats. Teddy was stretched out behind her, while another was lying in front of her, the gongadim's body much longer than hers. One was above her, curled up just above her head, while two more were sleeping by her feet. She hadn't felt this safe in a long time.

That last thought made her feel sad, like she was forgetting about Mummy and Daddy.

'So this is where my crew is,' Kemnebi announced.

All of the gongadims on the bed sprung to attention and sat up, including Teddy.

'Don't worry,' Kemnebi told them. 'You're not late for your shifts. I've just come to speak to our guests. I see you've met most of us now, Ayla.'

'Not really,' she replied. 'There was only Teddy here when I fell asleep.' She turned to her friend. 'Sorry, should I be calling you Sefu now?'

He laid a paw on her hip. 'No, I'll always be Teddy to you.'

'I better introduce you then,' Kemnebi said. 'The two grey and whites at your feet are Kosey and Shoshan. The tabby next to you is Lisimba, and his sister is behind you. Her name is Bubu.'

'Hi everyone,' Ayla said.

They all nodded and greeted her. Ayla still found it very strange to see their mouths moving like a human's mouth.

'Dakarai and Issa are flying the ship,' Kemnebi added. 'You'll meet them later. Come on crew, you have another hour until your shift starts, but I need to speak to Ayla and Sefu. Go on back to our cabin and finish your naps there.'

The four gongadims all stretched their front legs out in front of them, with their bums high in the air, before shaking their entire bodies and jumping off the bed. One by one they exited the cabin.

Kemnebi jumped up and joined Ayla and Teddy on the bed. Ayla smiled as he slowly spun around and kneaded the duvet with his paws, his claws catching on the material. 'So,' he said, 'from what Sefu . . .' He stopped spinning and looked at Ayla. 'Or Teddy if you wish.' He continued kneading for a few more seconds before sitting down. 'From what he's told us about your ship and its general location when it was struck by asteroids, we think we know which human space station the escape shuttles will have gone to.'

Ayla sat up in bed at the wonderful news. 'Really? How do we get there?'

'We'll take you there,' Kemnebi replied.

'Thank you, thank you, thank you,' she gleefully said.

'What is the name of the space station?' Teddy asked.

'I believe it's called FK2347,' Kemnebi told him.

Ayla spun around to look at Teddy. 'That was where the boomgaboons sold you.'

'It's not a problem,' Teddy said. 'It was a long time ago.'

'That's good because we're already on our way there,' Kemnebi said.

Ayla bounced up and down on her bottom, before shuffling on her knees over to Kemnebi and wrapping her arms around him. His fur was almost as luxurious as the duvet. 'Thank you very much,' she said, her face disappearing into his jet black fur.

Kemnebi glanced awkwardly at Teddy. 'Why don't I introduce you to Dakarai and Issa? I can show you the Ruby's bridge at the same time.'

Ayla released her tight grip on the giant gongadim and sat back on the bed. 'That would be lovely,' she said.

SPACE FOR A CAT

CHAPTER TWENTY TWO

A WHISKER'S BREADTH

J N WOOD

'How big is the Ruby?' Ayla asked as Kemnebi guided them through the ship. 'I couldn't see it properly on the space station. There was a lot of smoke.'

'She's not big but she certainly packs a punch,' he replied. 'The Ruby is a Class Three Transport vessel, with plenty of modifications.'

'ALERT! ALERT! CAPTAIN TO THE BRIDGE! CAPTAIN TO THE

BRIDGE! SCANNERS HAVE PICKED UP A BOOMGABOON SHIP!!!'

'**NOOOOOOO!!!**' Ayla cried. '**NOT NOW!**'

'Don't panic yet,' Kemnebi said. 'It might be nothing. It could just be a scouting ship passing by.' He had a quick glance behind them. 'We're closer to the bridge than your cabin now, so you might as well come with me.'

They started running, with Kemnebi in the lead. 'Does this mean we can't go to the space station?' Ayla asked.

'The captain won't know until we get to the bridge,' Teddy said. 'We'll find out what's happening soon.'

'I'm the unluckiest person in the universe,' Ayla whimpered.

'It might not be you,' Teddy said. 'It could be me.'

'It's not you, Teddy,' Ayla insisted. 'You keep saving me from the unlucky situations.'

Kemnebi took them up a ramp, leading them to the bridge. He pointed his nose at two chairs as he passed them. 'Strap into these seats,' he said, before bounding to the captain's chair and leaping up.

Ayla's bottom was almost on the floor when she sat on the chair. She'd almost forgotten she wasn't on a human ship, but then she noticed all of the chairs apart from the captain's were low down, just a few centimetres from the floor. The computer displays were also at a height easily reachable for a gongadim. Teddy was strapped into the chair next to her.

'Dakarai, situation report please,' Kemnebi requested.

A black and white coloured gongadim turned around. He was sat behind a display screen at the front of the bridge. 'One boomgaboon fighter ship heading our way,' he said, 'approximately two minutes out. They're not responding to communication requests, as usual. We are the only gongadim vessel for ten million miles, so we're on our own.'

'Can you tell if it's them again?' Shoshan asked as she entered the bridge, stopping near Ayla.

'Not yet,' Issa replied. She was a completely black furred gongadim sat on Kemnebi's right-hand side, but almost half the size of the captain.

'Is it the Barkle again?' Kosey asked as he entered. 'Why does that ship have it in for us?'

'We don't know yet,' Kemnebi answered, 'and they don't have it in for just us, they have it in for all gongadims.'

'Same thing,' Kosey said as he took his post.

'It is the Barkle,' Dakarai said. 'They're requesting comms. Shall I put them through?'

'That's not like them at all,' Kemnebi said. 'Let's see what they have to say.'

A crystal clear image appeared in front of them, showing a bridge full of dogs. They're boomgaboons, not dogs, Ayla reminded herself.

'Barkle to the Ruby,' a black furred boomgaboon said. She was laid out on top of a cylindrical platform, looking very relaxed, much more than she should have been considering the situation. She was surrounded by other boomgaboons, encircling the platform below her. 'This is Captain Darcey,' she said. 'Should we expect your immediate surrender? We don't want a repeat of last time. Do we?'

'No,' Kemnebi replied, his response drawing gasps of astonishment from his crew. 'We won't be surrendering,' he continued, instantly bringing relief to his fellow gongadims, 'not today or ever.' Kemnebi pressed a button on his chair and the screen vanished. 'All stations,' he sombrely announced, 'red alert.' He turned to Lisimba, who had joined them half way through Captain Darcey's surrender request. 'I think we should put our guests on an escape shuttle. We can't guarantee their safety, not after last time.'

'I agree, Captain,' Lisimba said. 'It's the only way.'

Ayla and Teddy shared a glance. 'Not again,' Ayla said.

'It seems so,' Teddy told her.

Kemnebi heard their brief exchange and turned to face them. 'I'm sorry about this, but it's the only way to keep you safe. The Barkle almost destroyed us last time. We managed to escape and limp back to Azibo, our home world, but we only survived by a whisker's breadth.'

'We lost more than a few lives that day,' Issa added.

'Lisimba will show you the way to one of the escape shuttles,' Kemnebi said. 'I'm not sure if the shuttle has enough fuel to make it there, but I'll transmit the coordinates of FK2347 to the shuttle's navigation computer. I'm sorry our meeting was so brief.'

'Will you be okay?' Ayla asked the captain.

'The Ruby has had a few more modifications since our last battle, so we have a few surprises in store for Captain Darcey and the Barkle.'

Ayla was scared to ask her next question as she unbuckled herself from the chair. 'Teddy,' she hesitantly said. 'Are you coming with me?'

Teddy did a double take while removing his safety belts, shocked by her question. 'What? Of course I'm coming with you. Why would you ask me that?'

'I didn't know if you'd want to stay with other gongadims.'

'I'm never leaving your side,' Teddy said. 'You're my family.'

'Follow me guys,' Lisimba said, before running down the ramp at the back of the bridge.

'Thank you for your help, Captain,' Teddy said as he followed Lisimba.

'It was no problem at all,' Kemnebi said. 'Stay safe.'

'Good luck, Captain,' Ayla said. 'It was nice to meet all of you.'

'Take care of each other,' Kemnebi called out as Ayla left the bridge.

SPACE FOR A CAT

CHAPTER TWENTY THREE

SAFE PAWS

J N WOOD

'SHUTTLE LAUNCH IN TEN... NINE... EIGHT...'

'Sefu, this is Kemnebi. There's no reason for the Barkle to come after you once you're jettisoned, but we'll draw them away if they do.'

'Thank you, Captain,' Teddy said as he sat down at the controls. 'I'll see you again on Azibo one day.'

'I hope so,' Kemnebi said. 'Safe travels.'

'THREE ... TWO ... ONE ... LAUNCH!!!'

Ayla was forced into the back of her chair once again. She was beginning to grow accustomed to her insides being shoved around and squashed together. Because the interior layout of the Ruby's shuttles were configured differently to human shuttles, Ayla was sat on a chair directly behind Teddy in the small cabin.

'Are you okay?' Teddy asked.

'I'm fine,' she replied. 'What are we going to do if we can't make it to the space station?'

'There's an inhabited planet on the way. The fuel we have should get us there.'

'And we definitely won't make it the whole way?' she asked.

'It's not worth the risk,' Teddy said. 'If we ran out of fuel we might just drift through space forever.'

'Who lives on the planet?' Ayla asked.

'I'm not sure. I don't recognise it, but its breathable atmosphere points towards enteenaps, gongadims or boomgaboons.'

'Let's hope it's not boomgaboons,' Ayla said.

'I wholeheartedly agree,' Teddy said as he watched the symbols and moving red dots on one of his displays. 'The Barkle is following the Ruby.

I don't think the boomgaboons even noticed us leave.'

'That's good. How long will it take us to get to this mystery planet?'

'Approximately two hours,' Teddy answered.

'Did you miss being able to talk for all those years?' Ayla asked.

'Of course I missed it, but I was never a big talker anyway, so it probably didn't affect me as much as you might think. It was frustrating at times, especially in the first few years.'

'Why didn't you write down a message so Mummy and Daddy would know who you really were?' Ayla asked.

'I can't write in human,' Teddy replied.

'But you speak English.'

'Very true,' Teddy agreed, 'but only because my vocal implant translates my language. I don't know how to write in human though.'

'I'm sorry the boomgaboons took you from your life like that,' Ayla said. 'It must have been horrible.'

'It was horrible at the beginning, but once your parents rescued me it became a lot better.'

Ayla tried to stifle a yawn but it forced its way out. 'I'm tired.'

'Try to get some sleep,' Teddy suggested. 'You're in safe paws with me.'

'I know I am, Teddy,' she murmured, as her eyelids suddenly felt heavier. 'I know I am.' A few seconds later she was fast asleep.

Teddy felt at home on the shuttle. It wasn't up to the standard of the space ships he'd piloted in the past, but at least this vessel was meant to be flown by a gongadim. Flying a human ship without opposable thumbs was difficult. The controls on this shuttle were designed for someone exactly like him.

He did a few checks on the planet they were going to land on. It was unregistered and nameless, meaning it hadn't been claimed by any species. He thought it might just be pirates down on the surface, but pirates still needed fuel, so hopefully they were friendly pirates.

SPACE FOR A CAT

CHAPTER TWENTY FOUR

DANGER IN THE SAND

J N WOOD

'Rise and shine,' Teddy announced. 'We've reached the planet.'

Ayla rubbed the sleep from her eyes. 'You should have woken me earlier. You must have been bored.'

'You needed the sleep. Hold on because it might be a rough landing. The scanners are picking up a chaotic weather system down there.'

'Would it be safer to find somewhere else?' Ayla asked.

'There isn't anywhere else. This is it.'

'I suppose we better land here then,' Ayla said.

'Yep,' Teddy agreed.

As soon as the nose of the shuttle penetrated the planet's outer atmosphere, everything began to violently shudder and shake.

'IS THIS NORMAL?' Ayla yelled. She could barely hear her own voice over the loud rattling noises.

'DON'T WORRY!' Teddy replied. **'I'VE FLOWN THROUGH MUCH WORSE!'**

It sounded and felt like the shuttle was going to start disintegrating around them. They suddenly, and very dramatically, dropped towards the planet's surface, the shuttle's nose dipping at the same time. Teddy struggled to regain control as Ayla let out a high pitched squeal. Lightning started striking the outside of the shuttle, the thunder filling their ears with incredibly loud crackles and explosive booms.

BOOOOOOM!!!
CCCRRRRACCCKKKK!!!
BOOM BOOM CRACK!!!

The thunder claps abruptly stopped and all they could hear was an irritating beeping, coming from somewhere in the shuttle.

Ayla was about to ask Teddy if they would be landing soon, when they were both forced forwards in their seats. They had hit something very hard. Then the shuttle was back in the air and their bottoms were no longer touching their seats. But again they lurched forwards as the shuttle crashed down into the planet. This time they were forced to stay in that position as the shuttle's nose carved a large ditch through the planet's surface. They eventually stopped, but that irritating beeping could still be heard.

'Ayla, are you okay?' Teddy asked.

'I think so. Are we on the planet?'

'We certainly are,' Teddy replied. 'Not a textbook landing, but I'm happy with that. We're still in one piece.'

'Can you call that landing?' Ayla asked. 'Didn't we crash?'

'I've crashed my fair share of ships, and that wasn't a crash. Come on, let's get out of here and find some fuel.'

Teddy slowly climbed out of his chair, double-checking that he wasn't injured. The landing had been rougher than he'd anticipated. He opened the hatch and a dry, hot wind nearly knocked him off his paws. A massive thunderstorm filled the horizon, but directly above them it was thankfully clear. Two fiery, bright yellow suns shone down on them. He noticed that with the wind came a lot of sand.

'I think we landed in a desert,' he said.

'Crashed in a desert,' Ayla corrected. She stepped alongside him as sand blasted her in the face. She squinted so she was able to look outside. Merely by habit, she started scratching the fur underneath Teddy's ear. He closed his eyes and leaned into her hand, until Ayla realised what she was doing and pulled her hand away. 'Sorry. Am I not allowed to do that anymore?' she asked. 'Do gongadims like that?'

'Pretend that nothing has changed,' Teddy said. 'Except for the fact that I can talk now. Over the years I've discovered that gongadims and cats must enjoy the same things.'

'Okay,' Ayla said, and pointed at lightning erupting from the black clouds in the distance. 'Did we just fly through that?'

'We certainly did, now let's get a move on. I don't want to spend too long on this planet.'

Teddy said he wasn't sure which way to go, but knew they shouldn't head towards the storm, so they started marching in the opposite direction. They were surrounded by dark orange sand dunes, so it was impossible to see anything beyond them. In order to make any kind of headway, Ayla had to lean quite heavily into the wind, so she was walking at quite an acute angle. The wind's direction would constantly change, causing Ayla to lose her balance quite often and fall to her knees. Teddy had a much lower centre of gravity so always managed to stay on his paws.

After they'd been travelling for thirty minutes, they both felt rumbling beneath their feet and stopped on the spot. Teddy scanned the tops of the dunes, searching for something big enough to make the ground beneath them shake. All he could see was orange sand whipping through the air, scraped from the sand dunes' peaks by the never-ending wind.

One of the giant sand dunes in front of them unexpectedly exploded. A ferocious roar soon followed, as a large, hairy beast erupted from the sand. It soared through the air for a brief moment before slamming back down to the ground, forcing more sand up to whip around them. The beast was huge, with hundreds of little fat legs along both its sides. It looked like a massive, hairy millipede, but with the head of an enormous rat. The beast was so big that Ayla was barely the size of one of the thing's stubby legs.

'RUN BACK TO THE SHUTTLE!' Teddy yelled. 'I'LL TRY TO DISTRACT IT!'

'I'M NOT LEAVING YOU,' Ayla cried. 'WE CAN RUN TOGETHER!'

The beast roared again and thrashed its ratty-head from side to side.

Teddy fixed his eyes on Ayla's. 'YOU HAVE TO GO! I'LL MEET YOU THERE!' He lifted his front paws up from the ground and tried to push her backwards. 'GO!' he shouted. His attention was drawn to the sand dune directly behind Ayla. 'What is that?' he whispered.

SPACE FOR A CAT

CHAPTER TWENTY FIVE

ERIC'S FLATULENCE

J N WOOD

Teddy watched in awe as something furry appeared over the brow of the dune. The first thing the gongadim could make out was a large head with long, dangly ears. Its gigantic body followed, with straggly fur that hung down to touch the ground. Two long teeth protruded from its mouth, very close to touching the sand at its furry feet.

Ayla had seen the same creature. 'Is that on our side?' she asked.

'I don't think there are any sides here,' Teddy replied.

The long toothed creature reared up on its back legs, letting out a strangled noise.

FLAAARRRGLAAARRRGLE!!!

It was running as soon as it had dropped back down onto all four limbs, heading straight for the hairy beast. The beast's attention was now fixed solely on the long toothed creature, preparing for the impending battle. Teddy nudged Ayla until she started moving. He didn't want them to be in the middle of the battleground when the two behemoths started fighting. The hairy beast was at least twenty times bigger than the long toothed creature, but both animals looked ready for anything.

As the long toothed creature passed them, Ayla and Teddy both noticed there was someone riding on its back. It was either a human or an enteenap, but it was difficult to tell because it was dressed head to toe in fur matching the creature's below. Ayla wouldn't have been able to tell the difference no matter what the person was wearing.

The hairy beast had stood its ground the entire time, not moving an inch. When the long toothed creature was close, the person riding it pulled back on its furry neck, forcing the creature to slow down and spin around. When the creature's very furry behind was facing the hairy beast, it released an almighty fart. The fur covering its behind was pushed out of the way so it was splayed in all directions, and the noise the massive trump created seemed to go on forever.

BUUURRRRRRRGGGGGGGFFFFFFLLLLUUUUUUPPPPPPFT!!!

The hairy beast took the expulsion of gas in its rat-like face. It drew its head back in revulsion, the pungent vapours easily penetrating the mass of hair filling its nostrils.

Teddy quickly lifted a paw to his nose, trying to block out the disgusting smell, while Ayla had her t-shirt pulled up to cover her face, neither of which entirely worked. Even though they were on the fringes of the powerful gas, and its strength was lessened slightly, they still struggled to stay upright.

The hairy beast roared its outrage, before spinning around and slithering away, its many legs propelling it across and through the top layers of sand.

'STAY WHERE YOU ARE FOR THE TIME BEING!' the rider of the long toothed creature shouted. **'THE AFTER EFFECTS OF ERIC'S FLATULENCE TAKES A FEW MINUTES TO DISPERSE!'**

Ayla and Teddy waited a full three minutes before exposing their faces. The lingering smell very nearly made them pass out, so they quickly covered their mouths again and waited another five minutes. They gingerly approached Eric and his rider once the winds had finally taken the stench away.

'Hello,' Teddy said. 'My name is Teddy and this is Ayla. We've come in search of fuel for our shuttle.'

The rider peeled back her furry hood and leaned over to get a closer look at Teddy. 'A gongadim eh? Don't see many like you around these parts.'

'We were forced to land here because we need fuel,' Teddy explained. 'Do you know where we could find some?'

'How much do you weigh?' the rider asked.

Teddy looked confused. 'Why do you ask?'

The rider tried to wipe the sand from the dry and wrinkled skin around her eyes. 'Oh, I was just wondering. I have some fuel at my camp and if I knew how much you weighed, I'd know how much you'd need. My name is Drit by the way.'

'But Drit,' Teddy said, 'you don't know where we're trying to get to.'

'That would have been my next question,' she told him. 'I bet you work out don't you? Lifting weights, that kind of thing.'

Teddy shot Ayla a confused glance. She looked equally perplexed. 'Not really, no,' he replied to Drit.

'You look nice and lean,' Drit said as she studied Teddy's body.

Teddy furrowed his brow and shook his head. 'Thanks, I think. We have things back at the shuttle. We could trade them for the fuel.'

Drit pulled her hood back over her head. 'Jump aboard. I'll take you back to my camp for some food first. After eating, we can load Eric up with the fuel and all head back to your shuttle. I'm sure I'll find something in your shuttle worthwhile to trade.'

Ayla turned to Teddy. 'What do you think?' she whispered.

'She did just save us from that huge thing,' Teddy said. 'Maybe we should go with her and find out what she's got.'

'Okay,' Ayla agreed. 'If we stick together we'll be fine.'

CHAPTER TWENTY SIX

FRESH GONGADIM

It was only after Ayla and Teddy were sat on top of Eric, did they worry about being so close to something that could create such a disgusting stench. They just had to hope the furry creature had some control over its intestinal gas releases.

Drit kicked with her heels and they started climbing up the steep incline of a sand dune. Eric's occupants rolled from side to side with each of the creature's long, lolloping strides. Ayla and Teddy gripped onto the fur beneath them, hoping the creature wouldn't be offended.

'How does Eric eat with those massive teeth?' Ayla asked Drit.

'She can't. That's why she's so obedient. Eric hails from another part of the planet where there's an abundance of craggy rocks. From a young age, she would have ground her front two teeth on these rocks, keeping them much shorter and more manageable. Without me feeding her, she would starve to death. It's the price she has to pay for having super-strong bottom burps.'

'So why is he here . . .' Ayla started to say. 'I'm sorry. Did you say Eric is a she?'

'That's right,' Drit replied.

'Okay, it doesn't matter,' Ayla said. 'Why is she here, with no rocks for her teeth?'

'I stole her from a herd when she was a little pup. My old mule died and I needed a new one.'

'You took her from her family?' Ayla asked. 'Why?'

'These mules are the only things that can fight the wind monsters, one of which almost had you two for dinner.'

'That's horrible,' Ayla glumly said.

'They are horrible,' Drit agreed. 'You think the smell that escaped from Eric was bad. The wind monsters could kill a whole city with their gases, if this planet had any cities left.'

'No,' Ayla said. 'Taking Eric from her parents was horrible.'

'Each to their own,' Drit scoffed. 'That's what I say. I won't judge you if you don't judge me.'

'Wouldn't it make sense for you to live where Eric comes from?' Teddy asked. 'I assume there are no wind monsters there.'

'My camp is here,' Drit replied. 'I'm not moving house for nobody.'

When they spotted Drit's camp a short while later, Ayla didn't think it was worth the risk that came with living amongst wind monsters. Located in the middle of a wide and deep valley, the simple camp was made up of a ring of six interconnecting tents, each one small with tattered old roofs. She was sure Eric would have had no problem carrying Drit's belongings back to wherever the creature had come from.

Eric carried them down the final sand dune and ducked under the rope connecting two of the tents, stopping when they were in the middle of the ring of tents. She dropped to her knees, allowing her passengers to disembark. There was a small fire burning in the clearing, with a large metal pot strung up so it hung over the flickering flames. Drit rushed to the fire to warm her hands, rubbing them together and showing her palms to the heat.

Ayla and Teddy both thought it was already too hot without the fire. Ayla couldn't believe Drit wasn't overheating wearing all that fur.

'Get comfortable around the fire,' Drit said. 'I just need to pop inside and prepare our meal.'

They watched her scuttle away and disappear into one of the tents, before Teddy leaned closer to Ayla. 'I don't trust her,' he whispered. 'You stay here while I go and see what she's up to. Talk as if I'm still here.'

'What shall I talk about?' she asked.

'Anything. It doesn't matter.'

'Okay,' Ayla agreed. 'Be careful.'

Teddy instantly turned into stealth mode, silently and gracefully slipping into the same tent Drit had entered.

'I really liked panka boom-boom,' Ayla loudly declared. 'What did you think, Teddy?' She paused for a moment, waiting for Teddy's imaginary response. 'Really? I thought it was delicious.'

Teddy could hear Ayla continue to talk about food as he moved around boxes and over pieces of rusty machinery. He made sure he was down low and out of sight as he followed the only sound within the tent. It was a strange scraping noise that Teddy couldn't quite place. But then he was able to follow Drit's voice. She was singing a strange song in a hushed tone.

*'My Pa-Pa, he'd go down to the mire,
The kids, they'd stack logs on the fire.
My Ma-Ma, she'd catch some gongadim,
Cook him on the fire, and eat him with a grin.'*

Teddy didn't like this song at all. Drit didn't have a very melodic voice, but it was the lyrics that particularly disturbed him. He peered over some crates and spotted Drit. She had her back to him, but he could see she was sharpening a long carving knife. He definitely hated the song. He turned around and made his way back to Ayla as quickly as he could.

SPACE FOR A CAT

CHAPTER TWENTY SEVEN

SAVING ERIC

J N WOOD

'We need to go,' Teddy whispered once he was back at Ayla's side.

'Why?' Ayla asked. 'What was she doing in there?'

'I'll explain once we're out of here,' Teddy replied.

'The food is almost ready,' Drit announced. She was walking across the clearing, making her way towards them. Her eyes were on Teddy as her tongue flicked out to lick her dry, cracked lips. Teddy was glad there was no sign of the carving knife. 'It's gonna be real nice,' she said. 'The last time I had this meal I was a little kid.'

'We're looking forward to it,' Teddy said, trying his best to act relaxed.

Drit pointed to a gap between two tents. 'I'm just gonna go and make a bit of room, if you know what I mean.'

'Don't worry about us,' Teddy said. 'We'll be here waiting.'

Drit danced away from them, her hips swinging beneath the furs. The twin suns were dipping behind a tall sand dune when she broke into song again.

'I'm gonna go poo-poo,
Down by the River Yuyu.
My poo-poo gonna go bye-bye,
While my eyes look up to the sky-sky.
Yeah, yeah, yeah!
I'm gonna do a massive poo-poo.

Gonna make some room for my din-din,
Gonna eat me some gonga...'

Drit loudly cleared her throat and slipped between the tents.

Teddy turned his attention back to Ayla. 'She wants to eat me,' he whispered. 'I'm almost certain she has no fuel. She just said that to get me here. We need to go.'

'What about Eric?' Ayla asked.

Teddy looked at the giant furry animal. 'I have absolutely no idea how to move an Eric.'

'Please Teddy,' she said. 'We need to save her from that woman. Eric is just like me. I know her parents will still be looking for her.'

'Okay,' Teddy sighed. 'Follow me. I think I might have a plan.' Teddy moved towards the same gap Drit had danced through.

'But that's where Drit went,' Ayla whispered.

'I know,' Teddy said.

Drit's voiced drifted across to them, dancing on the desert winds. She was singing another song.

'My poo-poo going down the shoo-shoo.'

Teddy spotted the fur covered woman squatting over a hole in the ground. He shifted his approach so they'd come up to her from behind. He turned back to Ayla to make sure she understood what his intentions were. She immediately nodded her head. Teddy was pleased to find a resolute expression on her face.

'So bye-bye poo-poo . . .'

Drit abruptly stopped singing, making Ayla and Teddy freeze on the spot.

'Who's that?' Drit asked, trying to look over her shoulder. 'Is that you Eric? How many times have I told you that this is my private time?'

Teddy took two quick steps and placed his paws on the woman's back, digging his claws into the fur. Ayla was only half a second behind him, grabbing Drit's furs from the other side of the hole. They pulled as hard as they could manage, but couldn't force her into the hole. Drit was a big and heavy enteenap, so they'd barely moved her at all. They knew almost instantly that they weren't going to be strong enough.

'WHAT DO YOU THINK YOU'RE DOING?' Drit angrily yelled. She tried to stand up with as much dignity as she could muster, considering the circumstances.

The sound of large, heavy feet thudding into the sand made Ayla and Teddy peer into the darkness. They moved out of Eric's way just in time, otherwise they might have been pushed into Drit's deep hole of a toilet. The tips of Eric's long teeth caught Drit on her belly, flipping the legs out from under the woman and turning her upside down. What goes up must come down, so Drit plummeted into her own excrement, landing face first. There was a loud splattering noise when she hit the putrid mess at the bottom, followed by squelching and sucking sounds as she tried to stand up.

'**ERIC!!!**' Drit shouted. '**GET ME OUT OF HERE YOU DUMB MULE!**'

Eric stepped back from the hole and turned to Ayla and Teddy. She crouched down, offering them a ride. They gladly accepted her offer and climbed up onto her back.

'ERIC!!! COME TO MAMA!!! SAVE MAMA FROM HER POO-POO!!!

Eric changed her pace from a trot to a canter, trying to escape her master's voice as quickly as possible. Ayla and Teddy held onto the fur beneath them for dear life. Eric took them around Drit's camp, away from the light of the fire and further into the increasingly darker night.

'Where are we going?' Ayla asked.

'I think I know,' Teddy replied, as he tried to steer the furry creature as best as he could. 'She's not responding to anything I do, but I'm pretty sure this is the way back to our shuttle.'

'What if Drit comes for us there?' Ayla asked.

'I doubt she'll be getting out of that hole anytime soon,' Teddy said. 'Judging by how long it took her to hit the bottom, it was a very deep toilet.'

Ayla grimaced at the thought of what it must be like down there. 'I bet it's disgusting.'

'Try not to feel guilty,' Teddy said. 'Think of what she's done to Eric, and what she wanted to do to me. Her family probably killed a lot of gongadims in the past as well.'

'Was she an enteenap or a human?' Ayla asked him.

'Enteenap.'

'What is the difference?' she asked.

'Enteenaps have a Triangulum feel to them, and humans have a Milky Way feel.'

Ayla shook her head in frustration. 'Anything more specific than that?'

'That's the only way I can describe it.'

It wasn't long before Ayla was climbing down Eric's fur in the pitch dark. Teddy was down on the sand already, inspecting their shuttle.

'Do you want us to feed you?' Ayla asked Eric, gesturing to her own mouth with her hand. 'A bit of food before you find your family?'

Eric spun around and ran away from them, disappearing over a dune or into the darkness, Ayla not sure which one.

'Will she be okay?' Ayla asked Teddy. 'Drit said she had to be fed by hand.'

'She'll be fine now,' Teddy said. 'She's going home.'

'I wish I could go home,' Ayla murmured.

'I think the shuttle can still take off,' Teddy told her.

'I thought we were out of fuel,' she reminded him.

'Almost out of fuel,' Teddy corrected. 'We have enough left to get into orbit. We can send out a mayday once we're up there and wait to be rescued.'

'Are we going now?' she asked. 'You must be tired, Teddy. I can't remember the last time you had a catnap.' She clapped her hand over her mouth. 'Sorry,' she said between her fingers. 'I said cat.'

'Gongadims also have a lot of naps, but they're not called catnaps,' Teddy told her. 'Our naps are called gonganaps.'

'In that case,' Ayla said, 'I think you need a couple of gonganaps.'

'I am exhausted,' he agreed. 'I only got a few hours' sleep on the Ruby.'

'Let's have a gonganap in the shuttle before setting off then,' Ayla suggested.

'Good idea,' Teddy agreed.

SPACE FOR A CAT

CHAPTER TWENTY EIGHT

WIND SURFING

J N WOOD

Ayla woke up because it felt like the shuttle was moving. She opened her eyes to find they were indeed moving. She assumed Teddy had taken off without warning her, but the gongadim was still fast asleep, curled up on his chair.

'Teddy,' she whispered. 'Teddy, wake up.' She realised there was no reason she should be whispering, so repeated the words much louder.

'TEDDY, WAKE UP!'

The gongadim opened one eye. 'Is it time to go?'

'We're moving,' Ayla said.

Teddy sprung up from his curled position and turned his display on. 'We are moving. I can feel it.'

'I know we are,' Ayla said. 'I just told you that. What does the shuttle say?'

Teddy studied the feedback from the external sensors. 'It says we're still on the planet. Well . . . actually . . . we're not on the planet. We're in the planet.'

'What does that mean?' she asked.

'We're fifteen metres under the planet's surface, moving in an easterly direction.'

'I still don't understand what that means,' Ayla said.

'Right at this moment, neither do I.'

A loud gurgling noise rippled around the shuttle, swiftly followed by another, and another after that.

Ayla looked up to the ceiling. 'What was that?'

'Unless I'm mistaken,' Teddy said, 'that sounded a lot like a rumbling stomach.'

'Are we under something alive?' Ayla asked.

'No,' Teddy replied. 'I think we're inside something alive, and it would have to be a pretty big something to swallow the shuttle.'

Ayla shuffled forwards in her seat so she could lean around Teddy's chair. 'A wind monster?' she whispered.

Teddy slowly nodded his head. 'A wind monster,' he agreed. 'Strap in. I think we're about to be expelled.'

'Expelled,' Ayla exclaimed. 'What does that mean?'

'This wind monster is about to go poo-poo down by the River Yuyu,' Teddy replied.

Ayla quickly pulled her safety belts over her shoulders. 'Are we going to be all right?'

'Don't worry,' he confidently replied. 'I'm right here with you. If we stick together we'll be fine.'

The gurgles started up again, soon turning into deep rumbles, like hundreds of huge fireworks exploding close to the shuttle's surface.

Ayla and Teddy were suddenly forced forwards, their safety belts holding them in place.

'WAAAAAHHHHHHHOOOOO!!!' Teddy jubilantly screamed.

'WE'RE GOING BACKWARDS!!!' Ayla yelled.

'IT DOESN'T MATTER!' Teddy shouted. **'THE WIND MONSTER HAS POOPED US INTO SPACE!'**

The shock from the sudden acceleration soon ended and they were very quickly, but quite comfortably, hurtling through space.

'Are we going in the right direction?' Ayla asked.

'Not yet,' Teddy replied. 'I'm waiting for the right moment to switch the engines on and set us on the path for the space station.'

'What are you waiting for?'

'I need to save some fuel for when we get to our destination,' he explained. 'Otherwise we won't be able to stop. If I change our direction at the right moment, I can switch the engines off and use the wind monster's wind to take us all the way home.'

'When do you need to do it?' Ayla asked.

'Right . . . about . . . nooowwww.' He pressed the button to switch the shuttle's engines on, but nothing happened. He pressed it again but still, there was no change.

'What's happening?' Ayla asked, the panic in her voice rising.

'Don't worry,' Teddy said. 'Probably just clogged up with a bit of sand. The shuttle needs a bit of time to clear its tubes.' He pressed the button and the engines roared to life.

'YEEEEESSSSSS!!!' he cried, punching the air with a paw.

Teddy used the engines to spin them around and guide the shuttle in the right direction. Fifteen seconds later, the engines were off and they were coasting through space.

'You did it,' Ayla said. 'Well done, Teddy.'

'Thank you,' he said, but his tone didn't sound like he was as happy as before.

CHAPTER TWENTY NINE

KLUBBA TIME

'Ayla,' Teddy said after a few hours of the shuttle coasting. 'Would you like the good news or the bad news?'

Ayla very loudly groaned. She was sick of bad things happening. 'Good news please.'

'There's a military grade enteenap ship ahead of us, and I reckon we should be able to get their attention.'

'Why is that good news?' Ayla asked.

'This is where the bad news comes in to play. I'm just going to say it quickly and get it over and done with. We don't have enough fuel to stop at the space station. After the engines didn't switch on straight away, I had to use too much fuel to get the shuttle on the right path. I've spent the last two hours trying to find a solution, but I can't find one.'

Ayla slapped her hands down on the floor next to the chair. 'I just want to see Mummy and Daddy again,' Ayla whined.

'I know,' Teddy said, 'and so do I, but the enteenap ship is our best bet now.'

Ayla crossed her arms and tucked her chin into her chest. 'We don't have any choice, do we?'

'No we don't,' Teddy replied. 'I'm sorry, Baby Girl.'

Teddy saying those last two words almost broke her heart. 'Okay then, Teddy,' she glumly said.

The military ship was still over an hour from their current position, but Teddy had to inform the enteenaps of their situation. He would only be able to slightly slow the shuttle down with the fuel they had left, so the enteenap ship would have to catch them at speed.

He put all of this information into a message and transmitted it to the military ship. He also provided the co-ordinates of their intended destination, and very politely requested a lift. The thirty minute wait for their reply was one of the most anxious times of his life.

'THIS IS CAPTAIN GUNNHILDR OF THE ENTEENAP SHIP, KLUBBA. OUR PLAN IS TO MATCH YOUR SPEED AND FLY ALONGSIDE YOU. ANY REDUCTION IN SPEED ON YOUR PART SHOULD COMMENCE NOW. PLEASE PREPARE FOR OUR

CLAMPS TO CAPTURE YOUR VESSEL.'

'Thank you, Captain,' Teddy said. 'It's good to hear your voice. My name is Teddy and my companion is called Ayla. I'll slow our shuttle down as much as I can now.'

'OKAY. SEE YOU ON BOARD IN FIFTEEN MINUTES.'

'Yes we certainly will,' Teddy replied. 'Ayla, that's excellent news,' he said as he switched the engines on and used up the last of the fuel. They felt the sudden decrease in speed for a few seconds, until the engines automatically turned off.

'What if the enteenaps won't take us to the station?' Ayla asked.

'Then we'll figure out a different way to get there. I'll get you back to your mummy and daddy if it's the last thing I ever do.'

'I don't want it to be the last thing you ever do,' Ayla said.

'I wholeheartedly agree,' Teddy said. 'My preference would be for us both to get home and live long, happy lives.'

'Okay,' Ayla said. 'Let's do that.'

SPACE FOR A CAT

CHAPTER THIRTY

STORIES FOR PANKA

J N WOOD

Teddy had been nervous during the build-up to the Klubba catching them. He knew how hazardous it could be clamping another ship at high speeds, but he hadn't wanted to let Ayla know how scared he was. When the Klubba's clamps had finally locked on to their shuttle, he had to stop himself leaping from his chair and dancing around in celebration.

'They have us,' he announced, trying to keep his voice calm.

'The first thing I'm asking is if they'll take us to the space station,' Ayla said.

'Okey dokey,' Teddy said.

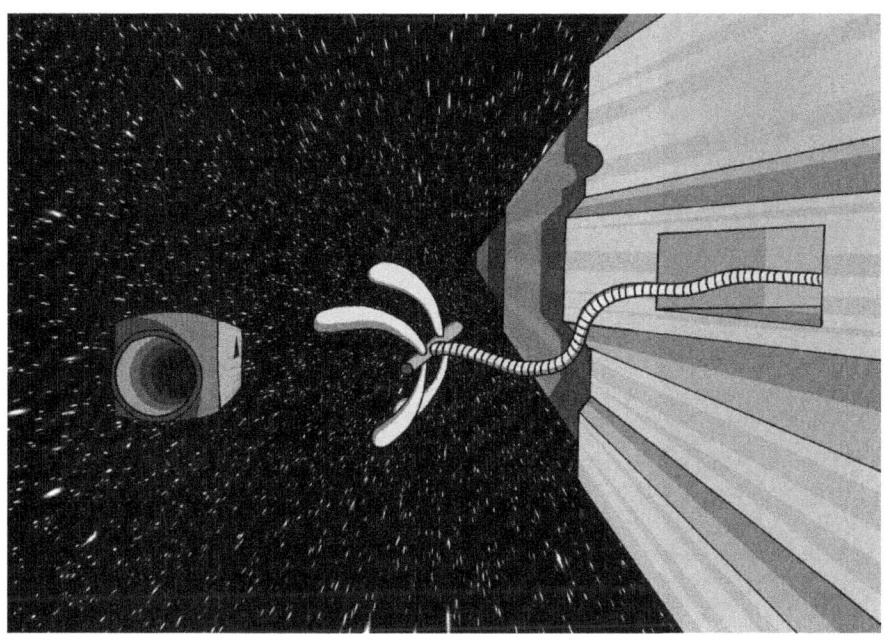

As soon as the shuttle was secured inside the Klubba, Ayla and Teddy were out of their seats and waiting at the door. It opened to a large docking bay. It was entirely empty apart from them, the escape shuttle and four smartly dressed, very official looking marines. Everything was a shiny grey, the floor, walls, ceiling, and even the marines' uniforms.

'Please keep your hands and your paws where we can see them,' one of the marines requested.

'Raise your hands into the air when you go outside,' Teddy told Ayla.

Ayla did as she was told, immediately lifting her hands above her head as she descended the four steps down to the grey metallic floor. When Teddy joined her, one of the marines approached them. Ayla thought she was very tall, and wondered if the enteenaps were generally a tall species. The other three marines were also tall, and Drit had been a big lady.

'I am Captain Gunnhildr,' the marine in front said. 'Welcome aboard.' She looked down at Teddy with her piercing blue eyes. 'You must be Teddy, a strange name for a gongadim.'

Teddy bowed his head slightly in greeting. 'It was given to me by my human family, of which Ayla here is a member.'

The captain turned her attention to Ayla. 'Yes, the lost human. We read Teddy's message detailing your story, and a very sad one it is. We will do our utmost to reconnect you with your  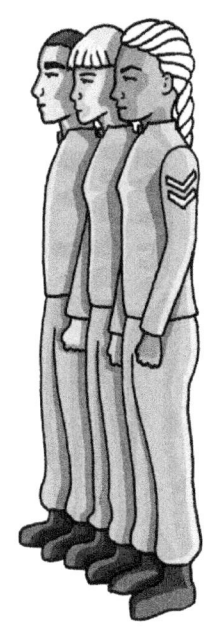 parents. We should already be on our way to the human space station known as FK2347.'

Ayla grinned down at Teddy before looking back to the tall captain. A single tear escaped her eye and rolled down her cheek. The crying was probably more from relief than gratitude. 'Thank you, Captain. We really do appreciate your help.'

'That's why we're here,' Gunnhildr said. 'Keep the peace and return lost strays, that kind of thing. Anyway, the Klubba is a very busy ship, so I must get back to work. You're free to explore, but for your own safety, I've assigned Corporal Viska to be your aide.'

One of the other marines took two steps forwards and stopped in front of them, her whole body as straight as an arrow. She had the shiniest hair Ayla had ever seen. She couldn't tell if it was silver or just a very bright white. It hung in one incredibly neat braid, going all the way down her back, swinging slightly when she walked. Ayla decided she would ask her mummy if she could also grow her hair that long and keep it in a braid.

'I hope you enjoy your brief stay with us,' Captain Gunnhildr added. 'It's only seven hours to FK2347 so we'll soon be there. Goodbye for now.' Ayla waved and the captain spun around on the spot. She strode past her marines and headed towards the large doors at the back of the bay. Two of the marines stepped into line behind their captain and followed, leaving Corporal Viska in front of Ayla and Teddy.

'So,' Viska said with a smile, 'for starters, you can call me Jess. What would you like to do first?'

Ayla glanced at Teddy before looking back up to the corporal. 'Well . . . I don't know about Teddy, but I'm really hungry.'

'I'm starving,' Teddy agreed. 'I'm so hungry I could eat a whole wind monster.'

'You've picked the best day to come aboard,' Jess said, 'because panka boom-boom is on the menu today. I doubt you've ever had that, Ayla.'

Ayla's smile filled her face. 'I have and I absolutely love it.'

'Perfect,' Jess said, before spinning around and following her captain's footsteps. 'Then follow me.'

Ayla and Teddy followed closely behind her, even more excited by the prospect of food.

'I hope a little human girl like you has never had the misfortune of seeing a real-life wind monster,' Jess said.

'We were eaten by one,' Ayla enthusiastically replied.

Jess glanced back to Ayla with one eyebrow raised. 'Really?'

'We were in that escape shuttle behind us at the time,' Teddy explained. 'If you check it over I'm sure you'll find teeth marks.'

Jess stopped suddenly and turned to face them, forcing Ayla's boots to slip on the shiny floor. 'You really were eaten by a wind monster?' Jess asked, almost beginning to believe Ayla's story.

Ayla gave the corporal one brisk nod of her head. 'And we were almost eaten by one when we weren't in the shuttle. A big furry animal called

Eric saved us. She was being ridden by a horrible enteenap called Drit.'

Jess looked to Teddy for confirmation. He merely raised his brows and nodded.

'In that case,' Jess said, 'I think you should tell me the full story of your time with the wind monsters. It's not very often that I meet anyone who has survived such an encounter.'

'If you can provide the panka boom-boom,' Ayla replied, 'I'll tell you my deepest darkest secrets.'

Jess let out a hearty laugh and opened the door behind her. 'I bet you do have lots of secrets, little human.'

SPACE FOR A CAT

CHAPTER THIRTY ONE

GONGADIM FIGHTER PILOT

J N WOOD

Ayla and Teddy sat in the middle of a huge canteen, surrounded by hundreds of tables, most of them occupied with tall marines. They had both happily accepted two servings of panka boom-boom, and were busy shovelling the second servings into their mouths. Ayla didn't think it was possible, but she thought the meal was more delicious than when she'd eaten it on the Santacruise.

Corporal Jess Viska listened with great interest to their stories, especially the escape from Blink's underworld dwelling and the planet full of wind monsters.

Ayla finished her last forkful and sat back in her chair. 'That was the best ever. I love enteenap food.'

'Have you ever tried oontullbootellbops?' Jess asked.

'That's what it's called,' Ayla exclaimed. 'I've been trying to remember its name. No I've never had it but I want to try it.'

'That's what we're eating later then,' Jess said. 'How about a tour of the ship? I can show you the sights.'

'Yeah sure,' Ayla said. 'Is that okay with you, Teddy?'

'I need a walk after all of that food,' Teddy replied as he rubbed his belly.

Jess started the tour by walking them through the ship's hydroponics bay, a wondrous place full of fantastic plants and trees. They were so strange and exotic that Ayla didn't recognise any of them from her school classes. Some of the trees were so tall they touched the very high ceilings of the bay. They passed under leaves bigger than some ships, and got up close to vibrantly coloured flowers, smelling the different array of scents.

The most beautiful flowers smelt the worst, some of them like rotting vegetables, while the less attractive ones seemed to have a much sweeter fragrance.

After the hydroponics bay, Jess took them to meet the rest of her squad, who were busy doing training exercises in the belly of the ship. The marines allowed Ayla and Teddy to join in with their hand to hand combat training. Teddy surprised everyone by overpowering a huge enteenap, at least three or four times bigger than the gongadim.

Jess allowed Ayla and Teddy to try on some fighter pilot helmets, and also taught them how to march like enteenap marines. While the corporal was congratulating Ayla on finally mastering the stride length, an incredibly loud and shrill ringing startled everyone, blocking out all other sound.

**BBBBRRRRRRIIIIIINNNNGGG!!!
BBBBRRRRRRIIIIIINNNNGGG!!!**

'What does that mean?' Ayla asked.

'It's the call to arms signal,' Jess explained. 'It means the ship has been requested to perform a task.'

'But we're so close to the space station,' Ayla said. 'It's only two hours until we get there.'

'Let's go and speak to the captain,' Jess told her. 'We can find out what's happening.'

Ayla and Teddy followed Corporal Jess Viska as she guided them to the bridge. They passed hundreds of other marines, all rushing to get to their posts. Jess stopped before an entranceway. The room beyond was a hive of activity, with marines striding back and forth.

'CAPTAIN, CORPORAL VISKA REQUESTING PERMISSION TO ENTER THE BRIDGE WITH TWO CIVILIANS!' she barked.

A small group of marines parted and the captain emerged from within. 'You may enter,' she responded, and waited for the newcomers to approach. 'I'm glad you're here,' she said. 'I'm sorry but your delivery to FK2347 will have to be postponed.'

Deep in her heart, Ayla knew the captain's words were coming, but she wasn't prepared for how demoralising they would be. Her shoulders slumped and her face dropped. She didn't have any energy left to protest. Teddy opened his mouth to speak, but the corporal beat him to it.

'But, Captain,' Jess said, 'we're so close. Can we find a little time to drop them off first?'

Captain Gunnhildr frowned at the corporal. 'The war between the gongadims and the boomgaboons has escalated dramatically, resulting in a number of skirmishes encroaching into enteenap space. As the enteenap's greatest warship, the Klubba has been recalled to enteenap space to assist in the de-escalation. We don't refuse orders, and lives may be lost if we hesitate.'

'Captain,' Jess said, 'what if . . . ?'

'Corporal,' Gunnhildr sternly said, 'you have always been an exemplary marine. Do not spoil your excellent record with insubordination.'

'Yes, Captain,' Jess briskly replied.

'If I may, Captain?' Teddy requested. 'Do you know what started the escalation?'

Gunnhildr switched her glare from the corporal to Teddy, her eyes softening by the time they'd met with the gongadim. 'A gongadim ship recently defeated a much larger boomgaboon ship. They took all of the boomgaboon crew as prisoners of war. We think the boomgaboon home world is embarrassed, so they're retaliating in a big way.'

'I don't suppose you know the names of the two ships concerned?' Teddy asked.

'Erm . . .' Gunnhildr said as she glanced behind her. There was nobody there to feed her the information, so she turned back to Teddy. 'I think it was the Ruby and the Barkle.'

Teddy smiled and nodded his head. 'Thank you, Captain.'

'Corporal Viska,' Gunnhildr said. 'Could you find these two some living quarters? I'm afraid they will be our guests for a little longer.'

'Do you know how much longer?' Ayla asked, her voice sounding as despondent as her face looked.

'Not just yet,' Gunnhildr replied. 'But as soon as I do know, you'll be the first human and gongadim that I tell.'

Ayla and Teddy followed Jess back through the same corridors, away from the bustling bridge.

Without turning to look at him, Jess said, 'Teddy, I know you have some piloting skills, but do you think you can fly an enteenap fighter ship?'

Ayla's eyes brightened as she looked at Teddy, waiting in anticipation for his response.

'I could fly one with my eyes closed and all four paws tied behind my back,' he insisted.

'Let's get you to a fighter ship then,' Jess said. 'I have a friend on the flight deck that owes me a massive favour.'

Ayla gleefully clapped her hands together.

SPACE FOR A CAT

CHAPTER THIRTY TWO

FAVOURS

J N WOOD

'That is a massive favour,' the rotund mechanic said. 'It's more than massive, it's a gargantuan favour.' The enteenap was nearly as tall as Corporal Viska, but he also had a round belly, bigger than a giant beach ball.

'I don't think it's anything compared to the time I saved your daughter from being eaten by a slatra beast,' Jess reminded him.

The mechanic slowly nodded his head. 'Yeah I suppose you're right. Launch bay seventy nine. She's all fuelled up and ready to go.'

Jess wrapped her arms around the enteenap, struggling to get all the way around his back because of his belly. 'Thank you, Bollr. You're a life saver.'

'Yeah, yeah, yeah,' he said, patting the corporal's shoulder. 'Now get these two out of here before I change my mind.'

'Thank you very much, Bollr,' Ayla said.

Bollr smiled down at her. 'You're very welcome.' He looked at Teddy. 'Make sure you return the fighter ship in one piece.'

'I'll even clean it,' Teddy told him.

They ran to launch bay seventy nine, receiving suspicious glances from everyone they passed.

Teddy reached the ship first and climbed the ladder to the cockpit, before lowering himself into the pilot's seat.

Ayla turned to Jess before she joined the gongadim. 'Will you get into trouble?' she asked the corporal.

'I expect so,' Jess replied, 'but I think you're worth it.' She dropped to one knee and pulled Ayla in for a tight embrace. 'I lost my mum and dad when I was your age, so I don't want the same thing to happen to you.' She let go and stood up. 'I know for a fact that Teddy will do everything he can to get you back to your parents.'

Now wearing a fighter pilot's helmet, Teddy lifted a paw and gave Jess a quick salute. 'Thank you, Corporal.'

'Good luck,' Jess said, and pointed up to Teddy. 'I'll see you, Fighter Pilot, when you return this ship.'

'You will,' Teddy agreed, as Ayla climbed into the seat behind him.

While Teddy was doing a few last-minute safety checks, Jess was fiddling with the security alerts so the fighter ship could launch without being detected. They didn't want anybody else knowing about their borrowing of a very expensive enteenap vessel. Captain Gunnhildr would find out eventually, but if Jess was successful, it wouldn't be until Ayla and Teddy were already safely docked at space station FK2347.

'Teddy,' Jess said over the radio, 'you are a go for launch. Whenever you're ready.'

'Thank you, Corporal,' Teddy said. 'Launch in three . . . two . . . one.'

The ship flashed across the launch bay, skimming a few inches from the floor. It slipped through the invisible force field, the only thing holding the atmosphere inside the launch bays, and rocketed into space.

'We are away,' Teddy said. 'Thank you and see you soon, Corporal Viska.'

Jess was no longer at the radio. She was already rapidly moving away from the launch bays, in case her presence alerted any more suspicion.

'Are we okay now?' Ayla asked. 'The captain won't try to get her fighter ship back?'

'I don't want to speak too soon,' Teddy replied, 'but so far we are undetected. I think they're too concerned about the Gonga-Boom War violating enteenap space.'

'That was good news about Captain Kemnebi and the Ruby,' Ayla said.

'It certainly was,' Teddy agreed. 'Maybe we will meet the captain one day on Azibo.'

'Does that mean you'll take me to your home world someday?'

'You're definitely going to Azibo with me,' Teddy said. 'I can't wait to introduce my human family to my gongadim family.'

'That would be amazing,' Ayla said.

'I'll take all of you, your mum and dad as well.'

'What if Mummy and Daddy aren't on this space station?' Ayla asked.

'We'll continue to search for them elsewhere,' Teddy replied. 'I'm sure Jess won't mind *tooooo* much if we keep this ship a little longer.'

CHAPTER THIRTY THREE

ANGRY LITTLE GIRL

J N WOOD

'Enteenap fighter to FK2347,' Teddy said into the radio. 'Are you receiving me?'

'Why aren't they answering?' Ayla asked. 'That was the thousandth time.'

'I'm not sure,' Teddy replied, 'and I think it was only the eleventh time I've tried.'

'It feels like a thousand,' Ayla said.

'Come on, Ayla. Where's the optimistic little girl I know so well?'

'I'm just so tired, Teddy. Everything keeps going wrong for us.'

'Enteenap fighter to FK2347,' Teddy repeated. 'Are you receiving me?'

'What do we do now?' Ayla asked, after Teddy's request was again met with silence.

'We're going to land inside this space station and find your parents.'

'But there's nobody here,' Ayla said.

'There's nobody answering our calls,' Teddy said. 'That doesn't mean there's nobody here at all.'

'What if there are people on here like Slink, Clink and Blink?' Ayla asked.

'There won't be, but if there are we'll avoid them. I probably shouldn't be telling you this, but I'm also a little scared of seeing the markets again.'

'It's good that you told me,' Ayla said. 'Now we can help each other get over our fears.'

They did a quick orbit of the space station, spotting a few other docked ships, so that meant there must have been some people still on the station. Teddy landed the fighter ship inside one of the many empty docking bays, finding the outer doors already open on arrival. Once the outer doors of the station had automatically closed behind them, they climbed out of the cockpit and made their way to the back of the small bay.

'We can't trust anyone,' Ayla said, as they waited for the docking bay's inner doors to open. 'Remember that Slink worked in one of these big docks.'

'We won't trust a single person,' Teddy said, 'only each other.'

'I love you, Teddy.'

'I love you too,' the gongadim replied.

The doors opened onto a gigantic room, similar in size to the huge dock on the first space station they'd visited, but this one was eerily silent and bizarrely empty. They couldn't see a single soul, not even one drone flying above them. There were no containers, no market stalls, not even the odd bit of rubbish on the floor.

'It's empty,' Ayla said. 'Mummy and Daddy aren't here.'

Loud snoring suddenly echoed through the enormous room.

'There's at least one person here,' Teddy said. 'Follow that snoring.'

In one corner of the massive, empty dock, was a man sat on a chair. He was leaning against the wall behind him, the chair's front two legs off the floor. Next to him were large double doors, with the word **EXIT** printed on the wall above.

'Excuse me,' Teddy said, causing the man to lean forwards, returning all four of the chair's legs to the floor.

The man loudly snorted, not hiding his annoyance at being woken up, before looking down at Ayla and Teddy. 'A talking cat,' he said. 'Well I never.'

'I'm not a cat,' Teddy replied.

'You certainly look like a cat,' the man said.

'He's a gongadim,' Ayla informed him. 'Do you know if anyone from the Aderinsola came here? It was an exploration ship that . . .'

'Yeah that ship's escape shuttles landed here a few days ago,' the man interrupted. 'What's it to you?'

Ayla bounced up onto the balls of her feet, her eyes wide with excitement. 'We were on that ship with my parents. Do you know how we could find them?'

'They probably came here,' he said. 'Doubt they're here no more.'

Ayla's excitement started to diminish as her hopes were beaten down yet again. 'Why do you say that?'

'This station is due to be deconstructed, starting tomorrow. Everyone is being shipped off somewhere else.'

'How do we find out if they're still here?' Teddy asked. 'Do you have a list of names?'

The man looked down at Teddy and laughed.

'**HA HA HE HE!** Talking cats are funny. Say something else big kitty.'

'**HEY!!!**' Ayla yelled. '**HE'S NOT A CAT! HOW DO WE FIND OUT WHO IS STILL ON THE STATION?**'

'Whoa there angry little girl,' the man said, taken aback by the outburst. 'Go down to security and ask them. They should know who is still here.'

Ayla's mood fell through the floor at the mention of the station's security. 'Thank you,' she angrily said. 'Let's go, Teddy.'

'Through the doors and turn right,' the man said as they walked away. 'You can't miss the security office. Hey, how much do you want for the talking cat?'

'Just ignore him,' Teddy instructed.

Ayla walked through the doors and turned left.

'He said right,' Teddy told her.

Ayla continued on her path. 'We're not going to see the security.'

'I'll go alone if you don't want to speak to them,' Teddy offered.

Ayla spun around to face him. 'You can't go. You heard that man asking if he could buy you. Humans are all the same. They'll want to sell you for food or display you as a circus act. And me? I'll be put to work in the tiny places that adults can't squeeze their giant bodies inside.'

'What do you want to do then?' Teddy asked.

'Can you help me look for Mummy and Daddy?' she asked. 'I'm going to search the streets.'

'Of course I can help you. I'll always be here to help you with whatever you need.'

SPACE FOR A CAT

CHAPTER THIRTY FOUR

MUMMY AND DADDY

J N WOOD

At the same time Ayla and Teddy were arguing about visiting the security office, Morrie and Kyra were on a cargo ship, arguing with the ship's captain. The ship was docked around the corner from Ayla and Teddy's borrowed fighter ship.

'You said we'd be leaving today,' Morrie said.

The captain checked his watch. 'Today isn't over yet.'

'What time are you planning on launching?' Kyra asked.

'Not until the time is right,' the captain replied, as he scratched his balding scalp. 'The station isn't empty yet, so I might get some more paying passengers before the day is out.'

'We paid you an extortionate amount of money two days ago to help us search for our daughter,' Morrie said. The anger rising within him was threatening to spill over into violence.

'And she'll still be out there if we wait another couple of hours,' the captain nonchalantly said.

Morrie closed his eyes and took a deep breath. He knew he couldn't hurt this abhorrent man. They needed him and his ship.

'She's a seven-year-old little girl,' Kyra said. 'We need to find her.'

'You've got a couple of hours until we leave,' the captain said. 'Why don't you do another search of the station?'

Morrie's eyes sprung open. 'What do you think has happened?' he asked. 'Do you expect us to believe she just flew herself into the station on a magic carpet?'

'Maybe,' the captain calmly replied, 'but you won't know either way standing here and talking to me.'

Kyra laid a hand on Morrie's shoulder, pulling him away from the infuriating man. 'This is pointless,' she said. 'Let's do another search of the station.'

Morrie turned to his wife and nodded. The frustration was fogging his brain and making it difficult to make decisions. He couldn't stand not knowing where Ayla was, or if she was even okay.

They left the ship and entered the empty dock, immediately heading for the exit and the docking master. They found him in his usual position, asleep on a chair. He'd been in that exact spot every single time they'd been to see him, which had been quite often.

Morrie kicked one of the front legs, forcing the man to thwack the back of his head on the wall behind him. 'Hey, wake up,' Morrie said.

The docking master opened one eye and peered at them. 'I think Captain Spongo's ship has some vacancies.'

'We already have passage on Spongo's ship,' Kyra told him. 'You know who we are.'

The docking master opened his other eye and looked them up and down. 'Oh yeah . . . the guys who lost their son.'

'Daughter,' Morrie corrected.

'That's the one. What can I do for you?'

'Have you seen our daughter or her cat?' Kyra asked, her tone turning as angry as her husband's.

'What does she look like?' the man asked.

Morrie huffed and groaned as he retrieved the photo from his pocket. 'We gave you a copy of this photo three days ago.' He held up an image of Ayla and Teddy. Ayla was smiling at the camera, while Teddy stared at her face.

'Hey, the talking cat,' the docking master exclaimed. 'I just saw them, maybe twenty minutes ago.'

Morrie and Kyra exchanged hopeful glances.

'You saw both of them twenty minutes ago, here?' Kyra quickly asked, as her eyes began to glisten.

'A talking cat,' the docking master said, shaking his head. 'Well I never.'

Morrie grabbed the man by his shirt heaved him up onto his feet. 'Where did they go?' Morrie desperately asked.

'Is there any reason why you seem to be manhandling me?' the docking master asked.

Morrie's eyes bore into the man's face. 'I'm really getting sick of your attitude,' Morrie growled. 'Tell me where they went, right now.'

'I sent them to the security office,' the docking master said. 'Now please unhand me before I have you arrested.'

Morrie pushed him back down so he sat on his chair. He grabbed Kyra's hand and they ran through the doorway marked **EXIT**, turning right towards the security office.

SPACE FOR A CAT

CHAPTER THIRTY FIVE

RELIEF

J N WOOD

'I ain't had your kid and her cat coming to see me,' the head of security told them. He was leaning back on a large leather chair, with his feet resting on his desk. 'I ain't had a visitor for . . . well my last visitors were you two. When was that, yesterday, the day before?'

'It was this morning,' Kyra said.

He looked surprised. 'Was it really? Well I don't know what young Kenny has been telling you, but he can't have sent them here.'

Kyra turned to her husband. 'Ayla might have got lost on her way here,' she suggested.

Morrie pointed at the man behind the desk. 'If our daughter and her cat come here, don't let them leave. We'll be back in an hour.'

The security man interlocked his fingers and placed his hands behind his head. 'Right you are.'

Morrie and Kyra left the office and started walking the empty streets, repeating their daughter's name.

Meanwhile, Ayla and Teddy were sat on the front steps of an empty, boarded up building, about half a mile from the security office.

'They're not here,' Ayla wailed. 'There's nobody here apart from that horrible man we spoke to.'

'We need to keep looking,' Teddy said. He nudged Ayla's arm with his nose.

'I'm going to sleep for a bit,' Ayla said as she rested her head on the hard concrete step. 'I'm so tired.'

'Okay, Baby Girl,' Teddy said. 'I'll wake you up in fifteen minutes. After that we need to . . .' He looked down at her face, seeing that she was already fast asleep.

Teddy needed to come up with a plan. He wasn't sure where else Morrie and Kyra could be. First of all, he needed to get Ayla off this station and find the Ruby. He knew Captain Kemnebi would help them. Failing that, he'd try to find the Santacruise. The last resort would be the Klubba, because he wasn't sure how helpful Captain Gunnhildr would be after he'd borrowed one of her fighter ships.

Teddy's ears perked up at the sound of voices. He hadn't heard anyone apart from Ayla for a while, so new voices were a shock. He heard them again, and it sounded like they were saying Ayla's name.

Teddy sat up straight, recognising the owners of the voices. 'Morrie and Kyra,' he whispered.

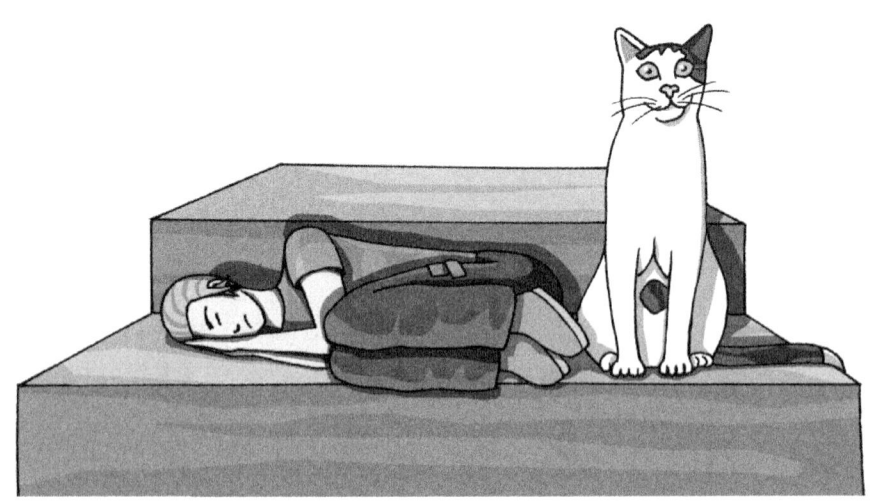

'AYYYYLAAAAAA!' one of the voices shouted, faintly floating through the space station's streets.

'That was Morrie,' Teddy said. He turned to Ayla and started padding her legs with his front paws. 'Wake up Ayla. They're here. I can hear Mummy and Daddy.'

Ayla moaned and pushed Teddy away, while Morrie's voice continued to get fainter and fainter.

'Stay here,' Teddy said. 'I'll bring them to you.' He leapt from the steps and sprinted across the street, following the voices and trying to pick up their scent.

'AYYYLAAAA!!!' Morrie shouted. **'TEDYYYY!!!'**

'TEDDY!!!' Kyra yelled. **'AYLA!!!'**

'Maybe that idiot docking master was lying to us,' Morrie suggested.

'Why would he lie to us?' Kyra asked.

'I don't know, because he's an evil and callous excuse for a human being.'

'He wouldn't lie about something so serious,' Kyra said.

'AYYYLAAAA!!!' Morrie shouted, his voice becoming hoarse from the strain. 'But it's a straight path to the security office,' he added. 'Ayla's a clever girl. It would have been difficult for her to get lost trying to find it.'

'MORRIE! KYRA!'

'Did you hear that?' Kyra asked. 'I'm sure that was someone saying our names.'

'No, I . . .' Morrie started to say.

'MORRIE! KYRA!'

'There it is again,' Kyra said.

'Yeah I definitely heard that,' Morrie said.

'HELLLOOOO!' he yelled. **'WE'RE OVER HERE!'**

'KEEP SHOUTING SO I CAN FOLLOW YOUR VOICE!'

'Who is that?' Kyra asked her husband. 'Is it the head of security?'

'No idea who it is,' Morrie replied. **'WE'RE NEAR MANSTAN BUTCHERS!'** he yelled, after reading the sign above an empty building.

'KEEP SHOUTING. I DON'T KNOW WHERE MANSTAN BUTCHERS IS.'

'WHO ARE YOU?' Kyra yelled. **'HAVE YOU FOUND OUR DAUGHTER?'**

'Yes, I came to this station with Ayla,' a deep voice said from above them.

Morrie and Kyra both spun around and looked to the top of the high wall behind them.

'It's fantastic to see you again,' Teddy said. 'Morrie, could you catch me please?'

'Teddy?' was all that Morrie could say, but habit made him hold his arms out, like he'd done for his cat many times before.

Teddy leapt into his waiting arms, almost knocking Morrie off his feet. Once he was held, the gongadim contentedly rubbed his face all over Morrie's beard.

'I'm here with Ayla,' he told them. 'Put me on the ground and I'll take you to her.'

Kyra hesitantly stepped towards them and stroked a hand down her cat's back. 'Teddy?' she asked with a quivering voice.

'Yes it's me. I'll explain the talking thing later. Do you want to see Ayla again or not?'

Morrie nodded his head, still unable to accept the fact that his cat was talking to him. He gently placed him on the ground, and then blindly followed when Teddy started running.

Teddy had to weave a complicated zig-zag of a route back to where he'd left Ayla. When he'd been looking for Morrie and Kyra, he hadn't used the streets, but he was aware of the fact that his human parents weren't as agile as him, so couldn't easily climb over walls and squeeze through the smaller gaps.

He turned the last corner, with Morrie and Kyra close behind him. He couldn't see Ayla, but assumed she'd just curled up and was out of sight.

'AYLA!' Teddy shouted. **'I'VE FOUND THEM!'**

As he approached the steps, with Morrie and Kyra crying behind him, Teddy still couldn't see her. There shouldn't have been anything near her that would block her, so he just hoped his eyes were deceiving him. When he was closer his heart dropped, as it was obvious she wasn't there. He quickly scanned the area, looking for any sign of her.

'AYLA!!!' Teddy screamed.

'Where is she?' Kyra asked. 'Teddy, where is she?'

Teddy was spinning around on the spot, desperately searching for her. 'I don't know. I left her right here.'

'MUMMY! DADDY!' a little voice called out.

Teddy, Morrie and Kyra all spun around in unison, finding Ayla at the other end of the street.

Morrie and Kyra started running, while all Teddy could do was close his eyes and let out a huge sigh of relief. He'd been certain somebody had taken Ayla, assuming he'd lost her to an evil human all over again. He took a few deep breaths to calm his nerves, before trotting to catch up with his human family.

Kyra reached Ayla first and scooped her up, before Morrie wrapped his arms around both of them. All three were loudly sobbing, unable to construct coherent words.

Ayla lifted her face away from Kyra's neck. 'I woke up . . . and . . . Teddy . . . wasn't there. I didn't . . .'

'He only left you to come and get us, Baby Girl,' Morrie told her.

'I missed you, Daddy,' Ayla cried.

Morrie held his wife and daughter, probably a bit too tightly. 'We missed you too,' he sobbed.

SPACE FOR A CAT

CHAPTER THIRTY SIX

TALKING CAT

J N WOOD

Ayla was safely held in her father's arms, while Teddy trotted along between Kyra and Morrie, purring so loudly the inhabitants of Earth might have heard him.

'Where are we going?' Ayla asked.

'We have passage paid for on a ship,' Kyra

replied. 'Now all we need to do is decide where it's going to take us.'

'I could do with dropping a fighter ship off with someone,' Teddy added. 'We had to borrow it so we could come here.'

'So . . . we have a talking cat now,' Morrie said.

'He's not a cat, Daddy,' Ayla insisted. 'He's the greatest gongadim in the galaxy.'

'I'll always be your cat,' Teddy said.

Kyra stroked a hand down Teddy's back. 'He brought our daughter back to us, so I think he's definitely the greatest.'

THE END

Printed in Great Britain
by Amazon